AMATEUR WINEMAKER RECIPES

AMATEUR WINEMAKER RECIPES

Edited by C. J. J. Berry

ARGUS BOOKS LIMITED

Published by

Amateur Winemaker Publications

Argus Books Limited
Wolsey House,
Wolsey Road,
Hemel Hempstead,
Herts. HP2 4SS,
England.

Cover Photograph by Nick Carman

Cartoons by Rex Royle

Some recipes by Cyril Shave

2nd Edition
First Impression September 1981
Second Impression December 1981
Third Impression September 1982
Fourth Impression November 1982
Fifth Impression May 1983
Sixth Impression March 1984
Seventh Impression August 1984

ISBN 0 900841 65 6

Printed in Great Britain by
Standard Press (Andover) Ltd., South Street, Andover, Hampshire
Telephone: Andover 52413

About this book

THIS book makes no pretence to be a detailed instruction manual, for that function is better performed by other books in this "AW" series – *First Steps in Winemaking*, a book for the beginner, *Progressive Winemaking*, *Scientific Winemaking*, *Common-sense Winemaking*, *Winemaking from Canned & Dried Fruit*, *Prize-Winning Wine Recipes*, and other manuals of more advanced winemaking.

All this book sets out to do is to record in a convenient form some of the more striking, successful and unusual recipes that have appeared in the *Amateur Winemaker* magazine in the course of a number of years, and which many readers have asked should be published in book form. Since they are intended to be a representative selection we have also included some of the more popular and commonly-made wines, so that the book covers a wide range of recipes.

With their help you will be able to turn out a selection of wines as appetising as they are different; and we hope you enjoy making them as much as you enjoy drinking them. It is hard to say which is the more delightful process!

C. J. J. Berry

Modern Winemaking

Nowadays thousands of people first take up winemaking through buying a "wine kit" in a chain store or home brew shop. Such kits are easy to use; one has just to follow the instructions on the label, rather like "painting by numbers", and many are quite content with this, as long as they are producing low cost wine of satisfactory quality.

Others, however, want eventually to take the hobby further, and to make wines from the fruits of their garden and the countryside, or even from purchased fruit, and the fact that there are today well over 1200 Winemaking Circles in the British Isles alone, to say nothing of those in Canada, Africa and "down under", each with a flourishing membership, is an indication of the extent of the modern revival of interest in this ancient craft.

Helping to promote and encourage this present day interest is the *Amateur Winemaker*, a monthly magazine with a circulation currently of over 20,000, selling throughout Great Britain, and distributed to enthusiasts in the U.S.A., Africa, and other countries as far afield as Japan and the Yukon. Many specialised books on the subject have been written by recognised authorities and other factors in the popularisation of winemaking have been the friendliness and infectious enthusiasm of home winemakers, and the willingness of education authorities to include the subject in their syllabus for evening classes.

Winemaking probably originated by accident when early man or woman first discovered the pleasant flavours and intoxicating effects of alcoholic fruit juices fermented by natural yeasts from over-ripe fruit stored in primitive containers.

Wine was certainly an everyday commodity to the ancient Egyptians, Greeks, Cretans, Romans and other Mediterranean peoples several thousand years before Christ. The Bible contains many references to vineyards, grapes, wine presses, bottles and wine. Noah is said to have been the "first" winemaker – and his story is a salutary one! – and wine became one of the essentials of good living, hospitality and merriment, as evidenced by the

Biblical story of Christ's miraculous provision of the wine deemed essential at a wedding feast.

Throughout the ages wine has been offered as a gesture of hospitality to one's friends and guests and somehow this aura of goodwill seems to embrace all winemakers too. Some prefer to work on their own, others appreciate the advantages to be gained by membership of a Wine Circle, where problems and recipes can be discussed, products sampled and comment invited, and speakers lecture on such diverse subjects as the history of glass bottle making or the effect of the sun upon the sugar content of fruit.

Wine Circles can also offer their members many social events and outings, and the advantages of bulk buying, saving heavy postal costs on individual parcels. If you wish to know the address of your nearest Circle write to: "The Amateur Winemaker", South Street, Andover, Hants. There is also a National Association of Amateur Winemakers, which organises an annual conference, a feature of which is a wine show which may have as many as 4,000 bottles exhibited.

Winemaking is certainly the "in" hobby of the 1980's. Some winemakers are content to make a few litres annually, others drink at least 4.5 litres (1 gal.) a week and give a lot away to friends as well; they might make 450 litres (100 gals.) a year.

Today, although all famous commercial wines (each with its own characteristic flavour) are essentially made from numerous varieties of grape grown in many different parts of the world, more and more amateur winemakers are learning to experiment and improve wines made at home from almost every type of fruit, grain, vegetable, leaf, flower and herb. These products now compare favourably with, and are sometimes vastly superior to, many commercial wines.

It is true to say that, thanks to the continual study, research and experimentation of recent years by many winemakers, including those with a scientific background and thorough knowledge of chemistry, yeasts and the processes of fermentation, winemaking knowledge has made big strides. Unlike other fields, in winemaking the experts' findings have been made available to the public in numerous books containing an introduction to winemaking and countless well proved recipes of interest to both the beginner and the expert. *First Steps in Winemaking*, published by the "Amateur Winemaker" is a typical example.

With only the simplest basic equipment anyone can produce wine of excellent quality, flavour and alcoholic content to suit palates of all tastes, from light dry dinner wines to rich sweet dessert and social wines.

Most of the utensils can be found in any kitchen – a large saucepan or kettle for boiling (stainless steel, aluminium, or sound enamel ware, but not iron, brass or copper), a large polypropylene "brewbin", a polythene bucket, bottles and corks, and a wooden spoon.

Other items which will be found useful are glass 4.5 litre (1 gal.) bottles or jars, fermentation traps to keep the wine from contamination, a metre (or yard) of plastic tubing for siphoning, a corking machine, a large plastic funnel for filtering (the larger the better) and, if you wish to go further into the "mysteries", a hydrometer to help calculate the strength of your wines.

Notice that your utensils, apart from the boiler and bin already mentioned, should be of glass, non-resinous wood (oak, ash or beech), food-grade plastic, or white glaze pottery (lead glaze can lead to poisonous results).

Everything must be kept scrupulously clean by the use of boiling water or baking in the oven, where possible, or by the use of a sterilising solution which can be used to rinse out bottles and apparatus. This is easily made by dissolving six Campden tablets and 10 g (¼ oz.) citric acid in 570 ml (1 pt.) of water. (Campden tablets are merely fruit preserving tablets).

Alternatively, you can use one of the excellent cleaner/sterilisers that are now on the market, such as Chempro or Silana PF.

Any wine consists of:
1. Flavouring,
2. Water,
3. Sugar,
4. Yeast, and
5. (hardest to obtain!) Time.

All that happens when yeast, a living organism, is put into a sugary solution, is that it feeds upon the sugar, converting it roughly half to alcohol and half to carbon dioxide, by weight, so that one finishes up with a pleasantly-flavoured alcoholic drink.

We extract the flavour from fruits and vegetables by boiling them, by soaking them in cold water, or by a combination of the two (i.e. pouring boiling water on them and leaving them to soak).

As regards sugar, one need only remember that 1 kg (2¼ lb.) to 4.5 litre (1 gal.) is required to produce a wine with sufficient alcohol to keep, 1.3 kg (3 lb.) will usually produce a strong dry wine, and more, up to 1.8 kg (4 lb.) will produce a wine correspondingly sweeter, since the excess sugar will not be converted to alcohol.

There are many types of yeast, and we would recommend either a good-quality wine yeast or a good granulated yeast. All will make wine, of varying quality, and usually the decision as to which type to use resolves itself into a matter of personal preference.

In all the recipes in this book use a wine yeast or 1 level teaspoonful of a good granulated yeast. With wine yeasts full instructions are supplied.

Beware of "No yeast" recipes. No liquor will work *without* yeast; it means that you are relying upon the natural yeast in the fruit, or, if you have killed that by the use of boiling water or sulphite, on any "wild" yeast which happens to be in the air . . . and the gamble may not come off.

Yeast nutrient can be used to "boost" the action of the yeast and is particularly recommended in flower, mead and other wines where the liquor is likely to be deficient in certain trace minerals. One can obtain nutrient ready made up and some yeast preparations such as Formula 67 include it with the yeast, but if you wish to make up your own it is sufficient always to use for each 4.5 litres (1 gal.).

½ teaspoon ammonium sulphate
½ teaspoon ammonium phosphate
1 Vitamin B₁ tablet (thiamine, or Benerva)

8

plus any acid required by the recipe. If none is specified use 2 level teaspoons of citric acid per 4.5 litres (1 gal.).

Wine, it should be noted, must have **some** acid, and also some tannin, for astringency, if it is to be correctly balanced.

The fermentation should be in two stages, the first vigorous one when the yeast is multiplying itself to the required level, and needs air for the process, and the secondary, quieter one, when it is converting sugar to alcohol, during which time air should be excluded; it is then that one should employ the device of a fermentation lock.

This will act as a barrier to the vinegar fly, and to the vinegar bacteria which are always a threat to the wine maker.

If they infect the wine it will turn to a peculiarly flavoured vinegar, fit only for the drain. In the early stages, therefore, the wine must also be kept closely covered.

Knowing all this, we can summarise the winemaking process thus:

1. Extract flavour from ingredients by boiling or soaking in bowl or crock.
2. Add sugar and yeast and ferment from 10 to 20 days in a bucket or fermentation bin in a warm place 17–25°C (65–75°F).
3. Strain off, put into fermentation jar and fit fermentation trap, filling to within an inch of bottom of cork. Temperature: about 15°C (60°F). This fermentation will be much softer and will proceed for some weeks, but eventually all bubbling will cease.
4. "Rack", i.e. siphon, the cleared wine off the "lees", or yeast deposit at the bottom of the jar. This should be repeated about a month later, and usually a third racking after a further three weeks is beneficial. By now the temperature should have been reduced to 15°C (60°F) and the wine should be quite stable, with no risk of explosions!
5. Bottle when wine is about six months old and corked securely. Bottles are then stored, on their sides, preferably in a room of about 12°C (50°F) temperature.

Do . . .

Keep things very clean.

Keep air away except during first few days, and even then keep brew closely covered.

Use fermentation trap for secondary fermentation.

Keep fermenting bottles full to within 25 mm (1 in.) of bottom of cork.

Strain wine well initially or it will be hard to clarify.

Keep a book and jot down all you do, so that you can repeat it.

Use new corks.

Don't

Allow vinegar flies to get at the brew.

Ferment in a metal vessel.

Put wine in old, damp bottles, or it may be infected.

Let sediment lie at bottom of bottle or it will impart a bad taste to the wine.

Rush a wine: give it time!

Forget to stir the "must" twice daily.

Use finings or filter unnecessarily; most wines will clear of their own accord, given time.

RECITS

RECIPES

(To make 4.5 litres (1.gal.) unless stated otherwise)

Agrimony and Banana

Ingredients:

450 g (1 lb.) fresh agrimony herb (or 55–110 g (2–4 oz.) dried
   herb) *(acrimonia cupatoria)*
110 g (4 oz.) dried bananas (or 900 g (2 lb.)) fresh bananas
   including skins)
450 g (1 lb.) raisins (sultanas, prunes, dates, etc., will do)
1.3 kg (3 lb.) sugar
15 g (½ oz.) citric acid (or 3 lemons, no pith, in lieu)
1 cup strong cold tea (or a pinch of grape tannin)
Water to finally make up 4.5 litres (1 gal.) of must
Yeast nutrient and activated wine yeast

Method:

Place the chopped herb and fruits together with the sugar into
the initial fermentation vessel. Pour in the *boiling* water and stir
well with a wooden spoon to dissolve the sugar. When cool add the
citric acid, strong tea, and yeast nutrient. Introduce the activated
wine yeast, and ferment on the "pulp" for 7 days, stirring the must
daily with a wooden spoon and keep it closely covered. Then strain,
for secondary fermentation, into a fermentation vessel and fit air
lock. Leave to ferment in the normal way, racking as necessary.

Agrimony and Rice

Ingredients:

1 small packet dried agrimony herb *(acrimonia cupatoria)*
450 g (1 lb.) fresh herbs or 55 g (2 oz.) dried herbs
450 g (1 lb.) wholemeal rice (or wheat, barley, etc.)
110 g (¼ lb.) raisins (or sultanas, currants and figs, etc.)
1.3 kg (3 lb.) sugar (or 1.8 kg (4 lb.) honey)
15 g (½ oz.) citric acid (or 2 lemons, no pith, instead)
1 tablespoon strong tea (or 3 g ($^1/_{10}$ oz.) grape tannin)
Water to make up 4.5 litres (1 gal.) of "must"
Yeast nutrient and activated wine yeast

11

Method:

Place the herb, grains, chopped dried fruit and sugar into the initial fermentation vessel. Pour 3.4 litres (6 pt.) *boiling* water and stir with a wooden spoon to dissolve the sugar, etc. When cool add the citric acid, strong tea and yeast nutrient. Introduce the activated wine yeast and ferment on the "pulp" for 10 days, stirring the "must" with a wooden spoon twice daily ensuring that the "must" is closely covered. Then strain, for secondary fermentation, into fermentation vessel, and fit air lock. Leave to ferment in the normal way, (after topping up to 4.5 litres (1 gallon), racking as necessary.

Other interesting rice wines are detailed in *130 New Winemaking Recipes.*

American Fruit Wine

American winemakers in California commonly make wines heavier in body than is customary in this country, where fruit is perhaps not quite so readily available in large quantities. They also commonly pasteurise. Here is a recipe – by Rockridge Laboratories, of Oakland, California – that readers might like to try:

FROM BERRIES

With berries like Strawberry, Raspberry, Loganberry, Blackberry, Boysenberry etc., use in these proportions:
4.53 kg (10 lb.) fruit, 1.7 litres (3 pt.) water
With currants, gooseberries and elderberries:
4.53 kg (10 lb.) fruit, 3.4 litres (6 pt.) water

Method:

Add fruit into enamel or stainless steel container, add the water, heat slowly, with occasional stirring, just to boil. Turn off heat, let fruit cool to room temperature (preferably overnight). Then drain through cheesecloth, collect juice in enamel or stainless steel container, or glass bottle. Press remaining "pulp" only lightly. Combine all juice in glass or wood container to prepare for fermenting into wine. Proceed about it as follows:

To each 4.5 litres (1 gal.) of juice, add

675 g (1½ lb.) sugar, mix to dissolve
1 crushed Campden tablet
1 yeast nutrient tablet
1 yeast starter (110 g (4 oz.) per each 4.5 litres (1 gal.) juice)

Ferment under sterile gauze or cotton cover, or use fermenting trap, at room temperature, 20–27°C (70–80°F). In 1–2 weeks, or whenever fermentation has ceased, let settle a few more days. Then rack clear wine into freshly cleaned bottles, full. Again let set upright, loosely corked, preferably in refrigerator at 2–10°C (35–50°F). When settled clear, rack off clear wine, sweeten to taste, heat in enamel or stainless steel container to 60°C (140°F), bottle hot, cap or cork tightly. Set aside to cool and age. If no sweetening in last step is desired, wine may be stored in full containers without pasteurising.

When quantity of fruit is too large to first make the juice as directed, the fruit is lightly mashed, water added as recommended. Then to each 4.5 litres (1 gal.) of mashed fruit/water mixture, add sugar, yeast nutrient, yeast starter, etc., as for the juice above, and add **double** the amount of sodium bisulphite, or 2 tablets (1 gm) per each 4.5 litres (1 gal.). Let ferment under gauze cover. When fermentation looks vigorous (1–2 days), drain all juice from "pulp", press only lightly. Combine all drained and pressed fermenting liquor and continue fermenting it under gauze or cotton plug, or fermenting bung, same as for fermenting the juice. Follow from here the directions as outlined for handling the wine from juice.

Apple Wine

Ingredients:

5.4 kg (12 lb.) mixed apples
1.1 kg (2½ lb.) sugar
4.5 litres (1 gal.) water
Yeast and nutrient

Method:

Make this wine in quantity, it is so easy. Measure out 5.4 kg (12 lb.) of apples, wash them quickly in running water in a colander, and then chop, mince, or pulp them. We use a crusher, but you can do the job with a piece of timber or half a brick in a tub, or use a mincer, but this last is rather hard work. Drop the pulped apple into a polythene dustbin and when you have done 5.4 kg (12 lb.) add 4.5 litres (1 gal.) of water. Then do another 5.4 kg (12 lb.) and add another 4.5 litres (1 gal.), and so on until your receptacle is full. Then add one level teaspoon of granulated yeast for each 5.4 kg (12 lb.), and stir well in. Cover closely and leave for seven days, stirring vigorously each day and pushing down the cap of pulp which forms to keep it wet. At the end of the week beg, borrow or steal a fruit press. Place a 4.5 litre (1 gal.) jar (as a measure) below the spout of the press and into the neck of it place a large funnel, holding a nylon sieve. Use a small saucepan as a "baler" and start filling the basket of the press with pulp and juice. The juice will run through freely, be strained, and gradually fill the 4.5 litres (1 gal.) jar. As each jar is full, plug it with cotton wool and stand it to one side, replacing it with another. Naturally, when the press is full of pulp, one starts pressing, and continues until the pulp is almost dry; then that pulp is thrown away and the basket gradually refilled.

Now count your demijohns, 4.5 litre (1 gal.) jars, and for each jar put 1.1 kg (2½ lb.) sugar into your dustbin, carboy, or other fermenting vessel. Pour in all the juice in the demijohns and add 1 level teaspoon citric acid per demijohn, and yeast. Stir well to dissolve the sugar. Fit fermentation lock and ferment, rack and bottle in the usual way. The wine is usually ready for drinking after about six months but is infinitely better if left in wood for a further year. And before someone points out to us that this recipe breaks all the rules we'll say "We know – but it always works!"

Apple and Raisin

Ingredients:

    **2.7 kg (6 lb.) mixed apples (or more), eating, cooking and crab
apples if possible**
450 g (1 lb.) raisins (or sultanas, apricots, etc.)
55 g (2 oz.) dried bananas (or 55 g (2 oz.) dried rose hips/shells)
1.1 kg (2½ lb.) sugar (or 1.5 kg (3½ lb.) honey)
10 g (¼ oz.) tartaric acid ("B.P." quality)
10 g (¼ oz.) citric acid (or 3 lemons, no pith, in lieu)
10 g (¼ oz.) ammonium sulphate ("B.P." quality)
10 g (¼ oz.) pectic enzyme
Water to finally make up 4.5 litres (1 gal.) of "must"
Activated wine yeast

Method:

Grate up the apples (including skins and cores) and place these
with the dried fruits and sugar into the initial fermentation vessel.
Pour in 3.5 litres (6 pt.) *boiling* water and stir well with a wooden
spoon to dissolve the sugar. When cool add the tartaric and citric
acid, ammonium sulphate, pectinol and strong tea. Introduce
the activated wine yeast and ferment on the "pulp" for 7 days,
stirring the "must" twice daily with a wooden spoon, and ensure
the "must" is closely covered. Then strain, for secondary fermentation, into fermentation vessel, top up with cold water, and fit air
lock. Leave to ferment in the normal way, racking as necessary.

Apricot (dried)

Ingredients:

450 g (1 lb.) dried apricots	**1 teaspoon of tannin**
15 g (½ oz.) pectolase	**Yeast and nutrient**
1 kg (2¼ lb.) sugar	**1 teaspoon citric acid**

16

Method:

Wash apricots well in hot water. Soak overnight in 2.25 litres (½ gal.) water. Next day bring to the boil and boil for five minutes. Lift apricots out carefully, strain into colander. Put all liquid in polythene bucket, cover well and place in a warm place. When cool, add pectolase, stir in sugar, put into demijohn, fill to shoulder with cold water, add tannin, acid, yeast and nutrient insert air lock and proceed as usual.

Apricot and Fig

Ingredients:

450 g (1 lb.) dried apricots
450 g (1 lb.) dried figs
450 g (1 lb.) sultanas (or raisins, currants, etc.)
55 g (2 oz.) dried bananas
10 g (¼ oz.) citric acid (or 3 lemons, no pith, in lieu)
280 ml (½ pt.) strong tea (or a pinch of grape tannin)
1 kg (2 lb.) sugar (or 1.3 kg (3 lb.) honey)
Water to finally make up 4.5 litres (1 gal.) of "must"
Yeast nutrient and activated wine yeast

Method:

Chop up the dried fruits and place these together with the sugar into the initial fermentation vessel. Pour in the *boiling* water and stir with a wooden spoon to dissolve the sugar, etc. When cool, add the strong tea, citric acid and yeast nutrient. Introduce the activated wine yeast and ferment on the "pulp" for 10 days stirring the "must" with a wooden spoon twice daily, ensuring that the "must" is closely covered. Then strain, for secondary fermentation, into fermentation vessel and fit air lock. Leave to ferment in the normal way, racking as necessary.

Artichoke (dry wine)

Ingredients:

> **1.8 kg (4 lb.) artichokes (tubers)**
> **1 orange**
> **1 lemon**
> **4.5 litres (1 gal.) water**
> **1 kg (2¼ lb.) white sugar**
> **225 g (½ lb.) raisins**
> **Yeast and nutrient**
> **1 cup cold strong tea**

Method:

Slice the artichokes and add the thin peel of the citrus fruit and the chopped raisins. Place all in the water and boil for 30 minutes. Strain the liquid over the sugar, stir well to dissolve and add the juice of the orange and lemon and a large cup of strong tea. Allow to cool, then add the yeast and nutrient. Leave two days closely covered, in a warm place, then put in fermenting jar and fit trap. Leave to ferment out, rack and bottle as usual. A sherry yeast seems to improve this wine.

Balm and Almond

Ingredients:

> **50 g (1–2 oz.) packet of dried balm herb (or 450 g (1 lb.) fresh herb)**
> **45 g (1½ oz.) bitter almonds**
> **55 g (2 oz.) dried banana**
> **450 g (1 lb.) raisins**
> **1.3 kg (3 lb.) sugar**
> **15 g (½ oz.) citric acid (or 3 lemons, no pith)**
> **280 ml (½ pt.) strong tea (or 3 g ($^{1}/_{10}$th oz.) grape tannin)**
> **Water to make up finally 4.5 litres (1 gal.) of must**
> **Yeast nutrient and activated wine yeast**

Method:

Mince the almonds and simmer in the water for 30 minutes: place the chopped bananas (and skins if fresh bananas are used), raisins, sugar and balm herb into the initial fermentation vessel. Pour on to these the hot almond liquor and almonds, stir well with a wooden spoon to dissolve the sugar, etc.

When cooled down to 20°C (70°F) add the citric acid, strong tea, and yeast nutrient. Introduce the activated wine yeast and ferment on the pulp for 10 days, stirring each day with a wooden spoon, and ensuring the must is closely covered.

Then strain into the secondary fermentation vessel and leave to ferment under the protection of a fermentation lock, racking as necessary.

Balm and Greengage

Ingredients:

1.1 litres (1 qt.) balm leaves, including stalks
900 g (2 lb.) greengages (stones removed)
450 g (1 lb.) wheat, barley or maize
450 g (1 lb.) raisins or sultanas
1.3 kg (3 lb.) sugar
2 lemons or oranges (15 g (½ oz.) citric acid may be used in lieu)
280 ml (½ pt.) cold tea
4.5 litres (1 gal.) water
Activated yeast and nutrient

Method:

Pour 850 ml (1½ pt.) of water over the grain and leave to soak overnight. Next day run the grain (being careful not to lose any liquid) and raisins through a coarse mincer, and put into crock with the balm leaves, chopped greengages and the juice of the lemons or oranges. Pour over them 4.5 litres (1 gal.) water of water *boiling*. Cover closely and leave for three days, stirring daily. Then strain add the cold tea, sugar, yeast and nutrient and stir thoroughly to dissolve the sugar. Pour into fermenting jar and fit air lock.

Ferment in the usual way and rack when clear. An excellent dessert wine with full body and attractive aroma.

Banana
(9 litres (2 gals.))

Ingredients:

1.3 kg (3 lb.) bananas	Water to produce 9 litres (2 gals.)
450 g (1 lb.) raisins	Yeast
2.7 kg (6 lb.) sugar	Yeast nutrient
1 teaspoon citric acid	

Method:

Peel the bananas before weighing them. Cut them up, together with the raisins. Then boil them in the water for about 15 minutes. Strain carefully, add the sugar, and allow to cool. When the temperature has reached 20°C (70°) add the yeast and allow to ferment 7 days before putting into a fermentation jar. Leave two months before bottling. Leave the wine six months in all before drinking.

For a different flavour, dates may be used instead of the raisins.

Barley

Ingredients:

450 g (1 lb.) barley	1 orange and 1 lemon
450 g (1 lb.) raisins	Yeast and nutrient
1.3 kg (3 lb.) Demerara sugar	Hot water to produce 4.5 litres
2 large potatoes	(1 gal.)

Method:

Put barley through mincer and then put it into a crock with the chopped raisins, scrubbed and chopped potatoes, fruit juice, fruit rinds (no white pith) and sugar. Pour over the hot (not necessarily boiling) water and when cool add yeast. Leave to ferment (closely covered) in a warm place for seven days, stirring daily. Then strain into fermenting jar, top up with cold water if necessary, and fit trap. Leave until wine clears and fermentation ceases, then siphon off into clean bottles and cork. This is a smooth dessert wine of about 14% alcohol by volume.

Barley and Apricot

Ingredients:

450 g (1 lb.) barley (wheat or maize)
900 g (2 lb.) dried apricots (or 2.6 kg (6 lb.) fresh apricots, stoned)
450 g (1 lb.) raisins (sultanas)
1.3 kg (3 lb.) sugar (1.8 kg (4 lb.) invert sugar)
10 g (¼ oz.) citric acid (or 2 lemons, no pith, in lieu)
280 ml (½ pt.) strong tea (or a pinch of grape tannin)
Water to finally make up 4.5 litres (1 gal.) of must
Yeast nutrient and activated wine yeast

Method:

Prepare the grains by soaking overnight and then by mincing them together with the dried fruits. Then place these together with the sugar into the initial fermentation vessel and pour in 4 litres (7 pt.) *boiling* water, stirring well to dissolve the sugar. When cool (20°C, 70°F) add the citric acid, strong tea and yeast nutrient, and introduce the activated wine yeast. Ferment on the "pulp" for 7 days, keeping it closely covered, and stir with a wooden spoon each day. Then strain into secondary fermentation vessel, top up, fit air-lock and ferment in the normal way, racking later as necessary. If fresh apricots are used they need merely stoning and cutting up – they should not be minced.

Barley and Grapefruit

Ingredients:

450 g (1 lb.) barley (wheat or maize)
3 or 4 grapefruits
500 g (1¼ lb.) raisins (sultanas or figs)
15 g (½ oz.) dried elderflowers (do not exceed this amount)
1.3 kg (3 lb.) sugar (or 1.8 kg (4 lb.) invert sugar)
15 g (½ oz.) citric acid (or 3 lemons, no pith, in lieu)
150 ml (¼ pt.) strong tea
Water to finally make up 4.5 litres (1 gal.) must
Yeast nutrient and activated wine yeast

Method:

Grind the barley and dried fruit in a mincer, having soaked the grains in 570 ml (1 pt.) of water overnight. Infuse the dried elderflowers, as in tea making, using 1.1 litres (2 pt.) of water, and bring to boiling point. Place the minced grains, dried fruit and sugar into the initial fermentation vessel, add the elderflower liquor, and the remainder of the water, which should be almost boiling. Stir well with a wooden spoon to dissolve the sugar, etc. When cool (20°C, 70°F) add the grapefruit juice and finely grated skin from one grapefruit (no pith), citric acid, strong tea and yeast nutrient. Introduce the activated wine yeast. Ferment, closely covered, for 10 days, stirring each day with a wooden spoon, then siphon, using nylon strainer, into secondary fermentation jar. Fit air lock and leave to ferment in the normal way, topping up and racking as necessary. This recipe permits much licence in variation of quantities of ingredients providing the dried elderflowers are not used in excess of 15 g (½ oz.).

Barley and Limeflower

Ingredients:

450 g (1 lb.) barley
55 g (2 oz.) dried limeflower
775 g (1½ lb.) figs (dates, sultanas or currants)
55 g (2 oz.) dried rose-hips/shells
1.3 kg (3 lb.) sugar (or 1.8 kg (4 lb.) invert sugar)
15 g (¹/₁₀th oz.) citric acid (or juice of 2 lemons)
15 g (¹/₁₀th oz.) grape tannin (or 1 cup strong tea)
Sufficient water to make up finally 4.5 litres (1 gal.) of must
Yeast nutrient and activated wine yeast

Method:

Wash the grains, then soak them overnight in 570 ml (1 pt.) of the water. The next day mince the grains in a domestic mincer, using the coarsest holes and then place the grains into the initial fermentation vessel together with the chopped fruits, bruised flowerheads and sugar. Pour on to these the *boiling* water and stir well with a wooden spoon to dissolve the sugar, etc. When cool (20°C, 70°F), add the citric acid, tannin, and yeast nutrient. Introduce the activated wine yeast and ferment on the pulp for 10 days, stirring each day with a wooden spoon, and ensuring that the must is closely covered. Then strain into the secondary fermentation vessel and leave to ferment under the protection of a fermentation lock, racking as necessary.

Barley and Orange

Ingredients:

450 g (1 lb.) barley (wheat or maize)
12 oranges (mixed sweet, Seville, etc.)
775 g (1½ lb.) raisins (or mixed dried fruits)
(280 ml (½ pt.) of grape concentrate may be used instead of raisins)
1 kg (2 lb.) sugar (or 1.3 kg (3 lb.) honey)
10 g (¼ oz.) citric acid (or 2 lemons, no pith in lieu)
140 ml (¼ pt.) strong tea (a small pinch of grape tannin)
Sufficient water to finally produce 4.5 litres (1 gal.) must
Yeast nutrient and activated wine yeast

Method:

Grind the barley together with the dried fruit (if used), having soaked the grains in 570 ml (1 pt.) of water overnight. Place the minced grains, etc., together with the sugar, into the initial fermentation vessel and pour in hot water. Stir well with a wooden spoon to dissolve the sugar, etc. When cool (20°C, 70°F) add the orange juice (and grape concentrate if used) and finely grated skin (no pith) from one orange, also add the citric acid, strong tea and yeast nutrient. Introduce the activated wine yeast. Ferment, closely covered, for 10 days, stirring each day with a wooden spoon, then strain into secondary fermentation jar. Fit air lock and leave to ferment in the normal way, racking later as necessary. If a full orange tasting wine is desired, add *after* the first racking one bottle of "curaçao" (red or white) or "orange" extract from the T. Noirot range of extracts.

Beetroot

Ingredients:

2.7 kg (6 lb.) beetroot	**1 lemon**
4.5 litres (1 gal.) water	**1.5 kg (3½ lb.) sugar**
Yeast	

Method:

Wash the beet, and cut them into slices, cooking gently in the water until tender, but not mushy. Strain on to the sugar and stir well to dissolve, then add the juice of 1 lemon. When cooled to blood heat add yeast and leave, closely covered, in a warm place for 24 hours. Then put into fermenting bottle, fit an air-lock and leave to ferment out. Bottle when clear and stable.

Red Fodder Beet

Ingredients:

1.8 kg (4 lb.) beetroot
4.5 litres (1 gal.) water
Yeast and nutrient
1.3 kg (3 lb.) sugar
110 g (¼ lb.) raisins
2 teaspoons lemon juice

Method:

Scrub the beetroot thoroughly. Cut off any green that may be left on them. Cut into thin slices and boil in the water until just tender. Strain off into jar containing the sugar and raisins. Stir for a few seconds until the sugar is dissolved. When cool (20°C, 70°F) add the yeast nutrient, and stir well. Leave for seven days, closely covered. Strain off into fermenting jar and fit air lock. The beetroot can be placed in jar containing half vinegar and half water, with salt to taste. (Makes excellent table beetroot).

Beetroot and Carrot

Ingredients:

    900 g (2 lb.) beetroot (young ones are best)
    900 g (2 lb.) carrots
    450 g (1 lb.) figs (or raisins, sultanas, dates, etc.)
    55 g (2 oz.) dried bananas (or 450 g (1 lb.) fresh bananas including skins)
    1.3 kg (3 lb.) sugar (or 1.8 kg (4 lb.) invert sugar)
    1 level teaspoon citric acid (or juice of 3 lemons)
    280 ml (½ pt.) of strong tea (or ½ teaspoonful grape tannin)
    Water to make up 4.5 litres (1 gal.) of must
    Yeast nutrient and activated wine yeast

Method:

Scrub the carrots and chop them up and simmer until tender in 2 litres (3½ pt.) of water. Scrub the beetroots and remove any green stalks, slice thinly and simmer in 2 litres (3½ pt.) of water. Place the chopped fruits and sugar into the initial fermentation vessel and strain into this the hot beetroot and carrot liquors (the carrots may be eaten) and stir well to dissolve the sugar, etc. When cool (20°C, 70°F) add the citric acid, strong tea and yeast nutrient. Introduce the activated wine yeast and ferment on the "pulp" for 7 days, stirring each day with a wooden spoon, ensuring that the must is closely covered. Then strain into the secondary fermentation vessel and leave to ferment under the protection of a fermentation lock, racking as necessary.

Beetroot and Clove

Ingredients:

    1.3 kg (3 lb.) beetroot (old ones are suitable)
    3 or 4 cloves
    450 g (1 lb.) figs (or raisins)
    1.3 kg (3 lb.) sugar
    15 g (½ oz.) citric acid (or 3 lemons, no pith, in lieu)
    A pinch of grape tannin
    Water to make up finally 4.5 litres (1 gal.) of must
    Yeast nutrient and activated wine yeast

Method:

Scrub the beetroots. Slice thinly and boil in 4 litres (7 pt.) of water until tender (not mushy). Place the chopped figs, sugar and cloves into the initial fermentation vessel and strain into this the hot beetroot liquor. Stir well to dissolve sugar, etc. When cool (20°C, 70°F) add the citric acid, tannin and yeast nutrient. Introduce the activated yeast. Ferment on the "pulp" for 7 days, stirring every day and keeping the must closely covered. Then strain into fermentation vessel and ferment under protection of a fermentation lock in the usual manner. Rack as necessary.

Beetroot and Cider

Ingredients:

1 litre (1 qt.) cider
1.5 kg (3–4 lb.) beetroot
450 g (1 lb.) raisins (or sultanas)
15 g (½ oz.) citric (or 3 lemons, no pith, in lieu)
A pinch of grape tannin
1.3 kg (3 lb.) sugar
Water to make up finally 4.5 litres (1 gal.) of must
Yeast nutrient and activated wine yeast

Method:

Scrub the beetroots and remove any green stalks. Slice thinly and boil in 4 litres (7 pt.) of water until tender (not mushy). Place the chopped raisins and sugar into the initial fermentation vessel and strain into this the hot beetroot liquor. Stir well with a wooden spoon to dissolve the sugar. When cool (20°C, 70°F) add the cider, citric acid, grape tannin and yeast nutrient. Introduce the activated yeast and leave to ferment for 7 days, closely covered, stirring the fermenting must daily with a wooden spoon. Then strain into fermentation jar, top up, and ferment under protection of a fermentation lock, racking as necessary.

Beetroot and Date

Ingredients:

1.8 kg (4 lb.) beetroot
450 g (1 lb.) malt extract
450 g (1 lb.) dates (or figs)
1.3 kg (3 lb.) sugar (or 1.5 kg (4 lb.) invert sugar)
15 g (½ oz.) citric acid (or 3 lemons, no pith, in lieu)
3 g ($^1/_{10}$ oz.) grape tannin (or 280 ml (½ pt.) strong tea)
Water to finally make up 4.5 litres (1 gal.) of must
Yeast nutrient and activated wine yeast

Method:

Scrub the beetroots and remove any green stalks. Slice thinly and boil in 4 litres (7 pt.) water until tender (avoid overboiling). Place the dates, sugar and malt extract into the initial fermentation vessel and strain into this hot beetroot liquor. Stir well with a wooden spoon to dissolve the sugar, etc. When cool (20°C, 70°F) add the citric acid, grape tannin and yeast nutrient. Introduce the activated wine yeast and ferment on the pulp for 10 days, stirring regularly with a wooden spoon, ensuring that the must is closely covered. Then strain into the secondary fermentation vessel and leave to ferment under the protection of a fermentation lock, racking and topping up as necessary.

Beetroot and Prune

Ingredients:

1.3 kg (3 lb.) beetroot
450 g (1 lb.) prunes
½ bottle Vierka concentrated must (or 1 litre (2 pt.) cider)
1.3 kg (3 lb.) sugar (or 1.8 kg (4 lb.) invert sugar)
15 g (½ oz.) citric acid (or 3 lemons, no pith, in lieu)
280 ml (½ pt.) strong tea (or ½ teaspoonful grape tannin)
Water to finally make up 4.5 litres (1 gal.) of must
Yeast nutrient and activated wine yeast

Method:

Scrub the beetroots and remove any green stalks. Slice thinly and boil in 4 litres (7 pt.) of water until tender (avoid overboiling). Place the chopped fruit and sugar into the initial fermentation vessel, and strain into this the hot beetroot liquor. Stir well with a wooden spoon to dissolve the sugar, etc. When cool (20°C, 70°F) add the citric acid, strong tea, Vierka must (or cider) and the yeast nutrient. Introduce the activated wine yeast and ferment on the pulp for 10 days, stirring each day with a wooden spoon and ensuring that the must is closely covered. Then strain into the secondary fermentation vessel, top up with cold water, and leave to ferment under the protection of a fermentation lock, racking as necessary.

Bilberry (dried)

Ingredients:

450 g (1 lb.) dried bilberries   4.5 litres (1 gal.) water
½ level teaspoon citric acid   Yeast and nutrient
1 kg (2¼ lb.) sugar

Method:

Bring the water to the boil and pour it over the bilberries and the sugar. Stir well to dissolve, adding the citric acid. Allow to cool to 20° (70°), then add the yeast and nutrient. Cover closely, and ferment in a warm place for seven days, stirring frequently to keep the "cap" of fruit wet and to prevent mould formation. Strain, then press the fruit and add this "run" to the other liquid. Put into fermentation jar and make up to 4.5 litres (1 gal.) if necessary with cold, boiled water. Do *not* throw the pulp away, but add to it a further 4.5 litres (1 gal.) of boiling water, a further kilo (2¼ lb.) sugar, and fresh nutrient and yeast, and obtain a second batch of wine, lighter in colour but still worthwhile, from the same fruit. (N.B. – Using this procedure, the addition of the fresh nutrient is all-important.) Often a third, and even a fourth brew can be obtained in this way, each progressively fermented, and siphoned into a fermenting jar. Thus one finishes up with two, three, or even four demijohns of bilberry wine, all of different colour and body,

28

and a year later it is possible to do some interesting blending to produce a red wine of exactly the type that one desires. Once in the fermenting jar, which should be opaque, or kept covered from the daylight to preserve the wine's glorious ruby colour, the wine is fermented, racked, and stored in the usual way. This is an easy wine to make in quantity, say 25 litres (5 gal.) at a time, if one has a large boiler.

Birch Sap

Ingredients:

4.5 litres (1 gal.) birch sap	**1.3 kg white (3 lb.) sugar (or**
2 lemons	**quart of honey)**
1 sweet orange	**1 Seville orange**
225 g (½ lb.) raisins	**Yeast**

Method:

Obtain a wooden beer or wine barrel tap, a piece of glass or plastic tubing, or even a piece of bamboo cane (with the pith removed). With a brace and bit of the same diameter bore a hole into the trunk of the tree just beyond the bark and insert the tap or tube, which should incline slightly downward to allow the sap to run easily. In March, when the sap is rising, it should be possible to draw off 4 litres (1 gal.) or so of liquor in two or three days. Plug the hole afterwards; if you do not the tree may die. Peel the oranges and lemons (no white pith) and boil in the sap for 20 minutes. Add enough water to restore the volume to 4.5 litres (1 gal.), then pour into crock containing the sugar and chopped raisins. Stir until sugar is dissolved; when cool add the fruit juice and yeast. Cover the crock with a thick cloth and keep in a warm place until fermentation has quietened. Then strain into fermenting jar and fit trap.

"I don't think you'll get it out any quicker"

Blackberry and Apple

Ingredients:

1.3 kg (3 lb.) blackberries   Juice of two lemons
1.8 kg (4 lb.) apples   Water: 4.5 litres (1 gal.)
1.3 kg (3 lb.) sugar   Yeast and nutrient

Method:

Chop the apples and put them with the blackberries and sugar
into bowl or plastic dustbin. Pour over them the water, boiling. Stir
thoroughly. Allow to cool, then add the yeast nutrient, yeast and
lemon juice.

Keep the vessel closely covered and stir the fruit each day to
make sure that all is kept wet and no moulds form. Ferment on the
pulp for a week, then strain into fermentation vessel and fit air
lock. Ferment and rack into clean bottles when clear.

Blackcurrant

Ingredients:

1.3 kg (3 lb.) blackcurrants   Water: 4.5 litres (1 gal.)
1.3 kg (3 lb.) sugar   Yeast and nutrient
1 teaspoon citric acid

Method:

Put the currants into a large earthenware jar and crush them.
Boil up the sugar in the water and pour, still boiling, on to the
currants. When it has cooled to about blood heat, add the yeast
(wine yeast or a level teaspoonful of dried yeast) and keep closely
covered for five days in a warm place, giving it an occasional stir.
Then strain into a fermenting jar, and fit an air lock. Let it stand
until fermentation ceases and the wine clears, usually in about
three months, then siphon off into fresh, sterilised bottles.

Blackcurrant and Raspberry

Ingredients:

   1.3 kg (3 lb.) blackcurrants
   450 g (1 lb.) raspberries
   225 g (½ lb.) malt extract
   80 g (3 oz.) dried rose-hips/shells
   10 g (¼ oz.) citric acid (or 2 lemons, no pith, in lieu)
   1.3 kg (3 lb.) sugar
   280 ml (½ pt.) strong tea (or 3 g $^{1}/_{10}$ oz. grape tannin)
   Yeast nutrient and activated wine yeast
   Water: sufficient to finally produce 4.5 litres (1 gal.) of must

Method:

Remove the stalks, etc., from the fruits. Place these, together with the dried fruit, sugar and malt extract into the initial fermentation vessel. Pour in the boiling water, and stir well to dissolve the sugar and malt extract, and also to crush the fruit, use a wooden spoon. When cool, add the citric acid, strong tea, yeast nutrient and introduce the activated wine yeast. Cover securely and leave to ferment seven days, then strain into fermentation bottles. Fit air-lock and leave to ferment in the normal way, racking as necessary in due course. Avoid using mildewed and overripe berries.

As a variation:

Use 900 g (2 lb.) blackurrants
    450 g (1 lb.) raspberries
    450 g (1 lb.) red currants or white currants
    55 g (2 oz.) dried bananas instead of rose-hips
    450 g (1 lb.) chopped raisins or sultanas instead of malt extract

Bramble Tip

Ingredients:

4.5 litres (1 gal.) bramble tips   Water to produce 4.5 litres
1.3 kg (3 lb.) sugar   (1 gal.) finally
1 teaspoon citric acid   Yeast and nutrient

Method:

Place the tips in a crock and cover them with boiling water. Leave is to stand overnight, then bring to the boil and simmer gently for a quarter of an hour. Strain through muslin on to the sugar, add the yeast when it has cooled, and keep closely covered in a warm place for 7 days. Then pour into fermenting jar, top up to bottom of neck with cold water, and fit trap. Leave until wine clears, then siphon off and bottle.

Broad Bean and Banana

Ingredients:

1.3 kg (3 lb.) shelled broad beans
450 g (1 lb.) bananas (or 55 g (2 oz.) dried variety)
225 g (½ lb.) raisins or sultanas
280 ml (½ pt.) strong tea (or 3 g ($^1/_{10}$ oz.) grape tannin)
1 level teaspoon citric acid (or 2 lemons, no pith, in lieu)
1.3 kg (3 lb.) sugar (or 1.8 kg (4 lb.) honey)
Yeast nutrient and activated wine yeast
Water: sufficient to finally produce 4.5 litres (1 gal.) of "must"

Method:

Simmer gently the shelled beans in 4.5 litres (1 gal.) of water for one hour. Use only beans that are too old for culinary purposes and be sure that the skins do not break, otherwise there may be clearing difficulties. Place the chopped bananas, skins and raisins, together with the sugar, into the initial fermentation vessel. Pour in the broad bean liquor and stir well to dissolve the sugar. When cool add the strong tea, citric acid (and 15 g (½ oz.) pectozyme if you wish), and yeast nutrient and introduce the activated wine yeast. Cover securely and leave to ferment for 10 days, stirring occasionally, then strain into secondary fermentation vessel. Fit airlock and leave to ferment in the normal way, racking later as necessary.

Celery and Apple

Ingredients:

    1.3 kg (3 lb.) celery (green portions included)
    1.3 kg (3 lb.) cooking apples (or 1 litre (1 qt.) cider)
    280 ml (½ pt.) grape concentrate
    1.3 kg (3 lb.) sugar
    10 g (¼ oz.) tartaric acid (E.P. quality)
    10 g (¼ oz.) ammonium phosphate (B.P. quality)
    Water to make up 4.5 litres (1 gal.) of "must"
    Activated wine yeast

Method:

Thinly slice the celery and grate the cooking apples, including cores and skins. Place these together with the sugar into the initial fermentation vessel. Pour on the *boiling* water and stir with a wooden spoon to dissolve the sugar, etc. When cool add the grape concentrate (or cider), tartaric acid and ammonium phosphate, introduce the activated wine yeast and ferment on the "pulp" for 10 days, stirring the "must" with a wooden spoon twice daily, ensuring that the "must" is closely covered. Then strain, for secondary fermentation, into fermentation vessel, and fit air lock. Leave to ferment in the normal way, racking as necessary.

Chamomile

The tiny, daisy like flowers of the chamomile plant, if you have the patience to pick enough of them, make an excellent dry wine, using this recipe.

Ingredients:

    2.25 litres (½ gal.) chamomile flowers
    1.3 kg (3 lb.) sugar
    1 teaspoon tannin
    2 lemons (or 1 level teaspoon citric acid)
    450 g (1 lb.) crushed barley, maize or rice
    4.5 litres (1 gal.) water
    Activated yeast and nutrient

Method:

Place the flowers and the crushed barley, maize or rice, grated lemon rinds (no pith) and sugar in the fermentation vessel. Add *boiling* water and stir to dissolve the sugar then leave to cool. Add the tannin, lemon juice or citric acid, activated yeast and nutrient. Ferment and rack in the usual way.

Cherry
Ingredients:

> **3.6 kg (8 lb.) black cherries (weighed whole and then stoned)**
> **4 litres (7 pts.) water**
> **1 Campden tablet**
> **1.5 kg (3½ lb.) granulated sugar**
> **Yeast and nutrient**

Method:

Wash fruit well. Crush it with a wooden spoon in a bowl. Bring 2.25 litres (4 pts.) the water to the boil and pour it over fruit. Crush the Campden tablet and mix it into two tablespoons warm water; stir it into fruit. Allow to stand for two hours. Boil remaining water and dissolve sugar in it. Pour sugar and water over fruit and stir well. Allow mixture to cool slightly, then add yeast. Cover the bowl with polythene and leave in a warm place for seven days for the first fermentation. Then strain mixture through muslin or nylon sieve into fermentation jar. Discard "pulp". Plug jar with cork and lock, and leave to ferment. When second fermentation has ceased, rack the wine and siphon it into bottles.

Cherry and Red-currant
Ingredients:

> **3–3.5 kg (6–8 lb.) cherries (any colour)**
> **450 g (1 lb.) red currants**
> **55 g (2 oz.) dried bananas or 82.5 g (3 oz.) dried rose-hips/shells**
> **225 g (½ lb.) malt extract**
> **5 g (¹/₈ oz.) citric acid (or 1 lemon, no pith, in lieu)**
> **120 ml (¼ pt.) strong tea or a small pinch of grape tannin**
> **1.3 kg (3 lb.) sugar or 1.8 kg (4 lb.) honey**
> **Yeast nutrient and activated wine yeast**
> **Water: sufficient to produce finally 4.5 litres (1 gal.) of "must"**

Method:

Macerate the fruits, ensuring no stalks are used, and remove the stones. Either the stones may now be discarded or the stones may be cracked (as in France) and placed in the "must". Add the dried fruits and malt extract and sugar, then pour in the hot water and stir to dissolve the sugar. When cool add the acid, strong tea, yeast nutrient and introduce the activated wine yeast. Cover closely and leave to ferment seven days (a Campden tablet may be used initially if desired); then strain into the fermentation bottle and leave to ferment in the normal way after fitting air-lock racking and topping up as necessary.

Variation:

1. A litre (a quart) of cider may be used in lieu of the dried fruits.
2. Use paddy rice with husks, barley or wheat grains in lieu of dried fruits.

Citrus
(18 litres (4 gals.))

Ingredients:

12 oranges	
6 Seville oranges	**This quantity for 18 litres (4 gals.)**
4 tangerines	
6 grapefruit	**Reduce proportionately for**
12 lemons	**less quantities**
450 g (1 lb.) sultanas	**Yeast and nutrient**

4.5 kg sugar (10 lb.) *will give the sweetness of a Sauternes*

Method:

Squeeze juice of all fruit into crock or polythene dustbin and add sultanas and 4.5 litres (1 gal.) of water. Pare very thinly the skins of a quarter of the fruit (no white pith) and pour on them 1 litre (1 quart) of *boiling* water. When cool add liquid to the tub containing the juice and throw the skins on the compost heap, add water to make up to 9 litres (2 gals.) and yeast and 2.2 kg (5 lb.) of the sugar.

"It's not *that* **dry!"**

Cover closely and leave for two weeks, stirring daily. Then add another 9 litres (2 gals.) of water and the rest of the sugar and leave until vigorous fermentation quietens down; rack off and put into casks or jars, fit airlock and proceed in the usual manner. Since Seville oranges and tangerines can be obtained only in January or February, two extra sweet oranges and two tablespoonsful of marmalade may be substituted. Sugar may be added in stages and quantities according to the individual's usual practice.

Comfrey

Ingredients:

5 Comfrey roots	**2 lemons or citric acid**
570 ml (1 pt.) strong cold tea	**2 oranges**
900 g (2 lb.) apples	**Yeast nutrient**
or 570 ml (1 pint) cider	**Yeast (selected wine)**
1.8 kg (4 lb.) sugar	
(or 1.3 kg (3 lb.) sugar)	
and 450 g (1 lb.) chopped	
raisins)	

Method:

Dig up and prepare by washing, peeling and cutting into fairly small pieces five Comfrey roots. Boil these in 4.5 litres (1 gal.) of water until tender, skim and strain on to the sugar, then add the grated apple or cider, the cold strong tea, lemon juice or citric acid. Orange juice and juice from the boiled lemon and orange peel (no pith). When cool stir in the yeast nutrient and selected wine yeast. Ferment on the "solids" for five days, then strain into fermentation jar, fit air-lock and ferment in normal way.

Concentrate (white)

Ingredients:

3 litres (½ gal.) Hildago grape concentrate (S.G. 1.400)
13 litres (3 gals.) water
30 g (1 oz.) tartaric acid
450 g (1lb.) dried apricots (chopped)

1.3 kg (3 lb.) white sugar
450 g (1lb.) Barbados sugar
450 g (1 lb.) glucose
1 large Bramley apple
Yeast and nutrient
2 Campden tablets

Method:

Mix 3 litres (½ gal.) Hidalgo's 1.400 grape concentrate with the water, tartaric acid, all the sugar and glucose 225 g (8 oz.) dried apricots (chopped) and Campden tablets. Set aside to ferment with a good wine yeast (or Hidalgo's dry wine yeast compound), air-lock is optional but keep well covered. After about 10 days, when fermentation is well proceeding *mix into the fermenting brew* one large Bramley apple and 225 g (8oz.) dried apricots, both previously pulped, then continue the fermentation process in the usual way. Ferment on the "pulp" for at least another 10 days, then strain. The above brew can be prepared from *red* or *white* concentrate. Variations may be made by adding to the fermenting brew, at any stage, 1.3–1.8 kg (3–4 lb.) of prepared *gooseberries, black-currants/berries, plums, raspberries, sloes, prunes, peaches.*

Concentrate (red)

Ingredients:

1 litre (1 quart) red concentrate
450 g (1 lb.) dried elderberries (or bilberries)
4 oranges (juice and pulp only, no peel)
40 g (1¼ oz.) citric acid
1 teaspoon grape tannin
4 teaspoons yeast nutrient
3.6–4 kg (8–9 lb.) sugar
Water for 8 litres (4 gals.)

Method:

Add near boiling water to all the above (suggest fruit in a nylon bag and use of a plastic brewbin) stir to dissolve the sugar, cover until cool. Add a working all-purpose wine yeast starter, fermenting 7–10 days, remove fruit and drain, rack the "must" in to a container, fit an air-lock and allow to work out – about one month – then rack.

Crab Apple

Ingredients:

4.5 litres (1 gal.) crab apples	**Yeast**
2 kg (3½ lb.) sugar	**Nutrient**
450 g (1 lb.) raisins	**Boiling water to make 4.5 litres (1 gal.) must**

Method:

Crush the crab apples in a bowl or tub and pour the *boiling* water over them. Stir and mash for 10 days, then strain. If you have a press, press the "pulp" and add the resulting juice to the rest. Stir the sugar in to the liquid and add the chopped raisins and yeast and nutrient. Cover the bowl closely and stand it in a warm place for 14 days for the initial fermentation then strain it in a warm place for 14 days and fit a fermentation lock. Rack into clean bottles when it is clear and the fermentation is complete.

Cups

CIDER CUP

Ingredients:

½ litre (1 pt.) cider	**Ginger and nutmeg**
½ litre (1 pt.) ale or beer	**1 wineglass gin or whisky**
Treacle or sugar	

Method:

Heat up the cider and ale and sweeten to taste with the sugar or treacle, then grate in ginger and nutmeg. Add gin or whisky and serve piping hot.

KENTISH CUP

Ingredients:

280 ml (½ pt.) sherry or fortified country wine	**2 oranges**
1 litre (1 quart) sweet cider or sweet white wine	**1 lemon**
	Angostura bitters

Method:

Put the finely grated rind of an orange in a punch bowl or jug. Add 280 ml (½ pt.) sherry, cover and stand for half an hour. Add the sweet cider (or any sweet white wine) and the juice of one orange and of a lemon. Stir and sweeten to taste. Just before serving add a thinly sliced orange and two teaspoons Angostura Aromatic Bitters. Serve chilled.

SUMMER CUP

Here is a novel "cup" for summer parties:

Ingredients:

1 bottle red or white wine	**2–3 lumps sugar**
1 glass sherry	**1 lemon**
2 bottles soda water	**A sprig of borage**

Method:

Chill the bottles of wine and soda water. Thinly pare the lemon rinds (no pith) and rub the rinds on to the sugar to remove the zest. Fifteen minutes before serving pour the chilled soda water and wine into a large jug, add lemon juice from half a lemon, the lemon flavoured sugar and the sherry. Add a little powdered sugar to taste and add the borage.

The flavour and strength will be agreeably varied if a liqueur glass of orange Curaçao and a few slices of orange are added. The amount of soda water may be reduced to give another variation. Avoid using ice in the jug; the bottle of wine must be chilled thoroughly. If only ice is available, stand the jug in the ice. Strips of cucumber may be used in lieu of borage.

APPLE CUP

Ingredients:

1 bottle apple wine
3 bottles grape wine or 4 bottles any good brew
480 ml (16 oz.) S.A. medium dry sherry
720 ml (24 oz.) Old English cider
300 ml (10 oz.) brandy

Method:

Why not try this recipe for a wine cup contrived by Lieut-Col. D. M. FitzGerald, of Five Chimneys, Friday Street, Eyke? He writes: I used one part apple to three parts red grape merely because that was what I had available. The colour was excellent and it looked good served out of a punch bowl (borrowed from the local wine merchant, no charge!) with mint and sliced lemon and peel floating in it. This should be sufficient for 40 claret glasses. The effect was excellent! It should be noted that all the ingredients are alcoholic. If something less potent is required tonic water, etc., could be used instead of, or as well as, cider.

PINEAPPLE COOLER (to make 40 wine glasses)

Ingredients:

280 ml (½ pt.) strong tea
140 ml (¼ pt.) lemon juice
420 ml (¾ pt.) orange juice
2 tablespoons lime juice cordial

225 g (8 oz.) sugar
1 tin pineapple slices
2 x 1 litre (4 x 1 pt.) bottles ginger
2 x 1 litre (4 x 1 pt.) bottles soda

Method:

Place tea, fruit juices, cordial and sugar in bowl. Put on ice or in cool place to chill. Just before serving add pineapple slices and juice, ginger ale and soda water.

Dandelion

Ingredients:

2 litres (2 qts.) dandelion heads
1 kilo (2¼ lb.) sugar
   1.3 kg (3 lb.) if a sweet
  wine is desired)

4 oranges
Water to 4.5 litres (1 gal.)
Yeast and nutrient

Method:

Pick the flowers when the sun is on them and they are fully open. Use the whole head (but not stem) and do not bother to pick off the individual petals, which is an exasperating and unnecessary chore. Pour the *boiling* water over the flowers and leave for two days. Boil the mixture for 10 minutes with the orange peel (no white pith) and strain through muslin on to the sugar. When cool add the fruit juice, yeast and yeast nutrient. Keep in a warm place, closely covered, for four days, then pour into fermenting jar and fit trap. Leave till it clears, then siphon off into clean bottles. This makes an excellent white table wine.

Dandelion and Burdock

Ingredients:

110 g (¼ lb.) dandelion leaves
110 g (¼ lb.) burdock leaves
  and burrs
Water to 4.5 litres (1 gal.)

1.8 kg (4 lb.) sugar
900 g (2 lb.) rice with husks
1 teaspoon citric acid

Method:

Boil the dandelion and burdock together in the water for 40 minutes, then strain on to the rice and sugar. When cool, add yeast and the juice of a lemon and cover closely. Stir each day for eight days, then strain into fermenting jar and fit trap. Rack into bottles when clear.

43

Dandelion and Raisin

Ingredients:

2–3 litres (2 qts.) flower heads (without calyx)
450 g (1 lb.) stoned raisins (or mixed dried fruit)
1.3 kg (1 lb.) sugar
15 g (½ oz.) citric acid (or 3 lemons, no pith, in lieu)
280 ml (½ pt.) cold strong tea (or a pinch of grape tannin)
Water to make up 4.5 litres (1 gal.).
Yeast nutrient and activated wine yeast

Method:

Discard as much as possible of the green portion of the flower (without being too fussy about it). Then measure the yellow heads and place these in a crock pouring over them 4.25 litres (7½ pts.) of *boiling* water. Cover the crock well and leave to soak for two days. Do not exceed this period otherwise harmful moulds may grow. Transfer the flower heads and resulting liquor to a boiler and bring to boiling point only. Meanwhile place the sugar and dried fruit into the initial fermentation vessel and strain on to the sugar, etc., the liquor from the flower heads and stir to dissolve the sugar. When cool add the strong tea, citric acid, yeast nutrient and introduce the activated wine yeast. Ferment "on the pulp" for 7 days, then siphon into fermentation jar making up the "must" to 4.5 litres (1 gal.) as necessary. Fit air-lock and ferment to a finish in the normal way, racking as necessary in due course.

Dandelion and Ginger

Ingredients:

450 g (1 lb.) of flower heads
15 g (½ oz.) essence cayenne
15 g (½ oz.) essence ginger
280 ml (1 pt.) cold strong tea
15 g (½ oz.) tartaric acid.
1.3 kg (3 lb.) sugar
Water to make up 4.5 litres (1 gal.)
Yeast nutrient and activated wine yeast

Method:

The whole heads can be used in this recipe if desired. Place the flower heads in a boiler, add the water and bring to *boiling* point only. Cut off heat and leave to infuse, as for tea, for one hour. Bring the liquor and heads back to *boiling* point only and strain the liquor on to the cayenne, ginger and sugar which has been placed into the initial fermentation vessel. Stir until sugar is dissolved. When cool add strong tea, tartaric acid, yeast nutrient and activated wine yeast. Fit air-lock and ferment in the normal way, racking if necessary.

Dandelion and Rice

Ingredients:

2–3 litres (2–3 qts.) flower heads (with calyx)
900 g (2 lb.) paddy rice (with husk)
450 g (1 lb.) stoned raisins (or mixed dried fruit)
1.3 kg (3 lb.) sugar
15 g (½ oz.) citric acid (or 3 lemons, no pith, in lieu)
280 ml (½ pt.) cold strong tea (or a inch of grape tannin)
Water to 4.5 litres (1 gal.)
Yeast nutrient and activated wine yeast

Method:

Prepare and measure the flower heads, discarding as much as possible of the green part of the flower head. Place flower heads in polythene bucket or crock and pour over them 4.25 litres (7½ pts.) *boiling* water. Cover the vessel well and leave to soak for 48 hours (no longer). Transfer the flower heads and liquor into a saucepan or boiler and bring to boiling point only. Place the sugar, paddy rice and raisins into the initial fermentation vessel then pour in the strained flower head liquor and stir to dissolve the sugar. When cool add the cold strong tea, citric acid, yeast nutrient and introduce the activated wine yeast; ferment on the "pulp" for 7 days. Then siphon into fermentation jar, making up to 4.5 litres (1 gal.) if necessary. Fit air-lock and ferment to a finish in the normal way. Rack as necessary.

Dandelion and Rosehip

Ingredients:

2–3 litres (2–3 qts.) of flower heads (without calyx)
225 g (8 oz.) dried rose-hips or
110 g (4 oz.) rose-hip/shells (a handful of dried elder-
　berries or bilberries will give this wine an excellent colour)
1.5 kg (3½ lb.) sugar
15 g (½ oz.) citric acid (or 3 lemons, no pith, in lieu)
280 ml (½ pt.) cold strong tea (or a pinch of grape tannin)
Water
Yeast nutrient and activated wine yeast

Method:

Measure the flower heads from which almost all the green portion has been removed. Place the flower heads in a crock or plastic vessel and cover with 4.25 litres (7½ pts.) of *boiling* water and cover well, leaving to soak for 48 hours (no longer). Transfer the flowers and liquor to a boiler or saucepan and heat to boiling point only. Place the sugar and rose-hips into the initial fermentation vessel and strain on to these the liquor from the flower heads. Stir to dissolve the sugar. When cool add the strong tea, citric acid, yeast nutrient and introduce the activated wine yeast. Ferment on the "pulp" for 7 days (450 g (1 lb.) dried fruit can be added with advantage). Then siphon into fermentation jar making up the "must" to 4.5 litres (1 gal.) if necessary. Fit air-lock and ferment to a finish in the normal way, racking as necessary.

Dandelion and Fig

Ingredients:

2–3 litres (2–3 qts.) of flower heads (without calyx)
900 g (2 lb.) dried figs
1.3 kg (3 lb.) sugar
15 g (½ oz.) citric acid (or 3 lemons, no pith, in lieu)
280 ml (½ pt.) cold strong tea (or a pinch of grape tannin)
Water to make up 4.5 litres (1 gal.)
Yeast nutrient and activated wine yeast

Method:

Prepare and measure the flower heads. Bring the water to *boiling* point and add the flower heads. Leave for one hour to infuse as in tea making, then bring liquor up to boiling point once again, and strain this liquor on to the chopped figs and sugar which have been placed into the initial fermentation vessel, and stir to dissolve the sugar. When cool add the strong tea, citric acid, yeast nutrient and introduce the activated wine yeast. Ferment on the "pulp" for 7 days, then siphon into fermentation jar making up the "must" to 4.5 litres (1 gal.) if necessary. Fit air-lock and ferment to a finish in the normal way, racking as necessary.

Dandelion and Prune

Ingredients:

    2–3 litres (2–3 qts.) flower heads
    450 g (1 lb.) prunes (other dried fruits can be used, in lieu)
    450 g (1 lb.) honey (if available)
    1 Bottle Ribena Blackcurrant juice
    1.1 kg (2½ lb.) sugar (use 1.3 kg) of sugar if honey is not used)
    570 ml (1 pt.) cold strong tea
    15 g (½ oz.) citric acid (or 3 lemons, no pith, in lieu)
    Water to make up 4.5 litres (1 gal.)
    Yeast nutrient and activated wine yeast

Method:

Place the whole heads in a boiler, add water and bring to *boiling* point only. Cut off the heat and leave to infuse for one hour (as for making tea). Bring the liquor with flower heads back to boiling point only, then strain this liquor on to the chopped prunes and sugar in the initial fermentation vessel. Stir well to dissolve sugar. When lukewarm stir in honey and leave to cool, then add the Ribena, strong tea, citric acid, yeast nutrient and activated wine yeast. Keep well covered for 7 days, then siphon into fermentation jar, air-lock, and ferment to a finish in the normal way, rack as necessary.

Date (dry)

Ingredients:

1.8 kg (4 lb.) dates	**Juice of 4 lemons**
225 g (½ lb.) sugar	**Yeast and nutrient**
1 teaspoon tannin	

Method:

The dates should be chopped and slowly boiled with 225 g (½ lb.) of sugar in 4.5 litres (1 gal.) of water for half an hour.

Ample sugar will then have been extracted from them. It helps to add a few date stones during the boiling to impart a very slight bitterness to give the wine zest.

When the liquid has cooled, strain, and add the rind and juice, the lemons, the yeast and yeast nutrient, and ferment under an air lock in the usual way. When the wine fully clears, rack and mature for six months. This is best made as a sweet dessert wine and the fermentation can often be prolonged by "feeding" with small dose of sugar, adding 110 g (4 oz.) each time the S.G. has dropped to 1,000.

Date (sweet)

(Medium sweet, Cream Sherry type wine)

Ingredients:

1.8 kg (4 lb.) dates	**1 teaspoon tannin**
900 g (2 lb.) sugar	**2 large lemons**
Water to 4.5 litres (1 gal.)	**1 orange**
1 grapefruit	**Sherry yeast and nutrient**

Method:

Chop and boil the dates gently for half an hour with the rinds of the fruit (leave half a dozen of the date stones in the saucepan but omit the others). Strain on to the sugar, add the fruit juice, and stir well to dissolve. When cool add the yeast and nutrient, put into fermentation jar and fit trap. Ferment out, adding sugar in 110 g (4 oz.) lots towards the end of the fermentation, as necessary, each time gravity reaches 1,000.

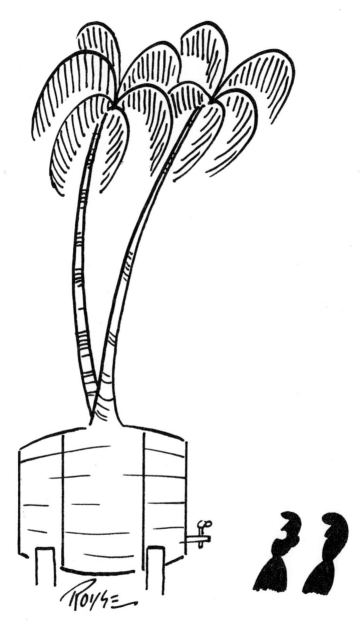

"Fancy a drop of date?"

Elderberry (dried)

Ingredients:

225 g (½ lb.) dried elderberries
450 g (1 lb.) of raisins
1 good teaspoonful of citric acid
1.3 kg (3 lb.) sugar
Yeast and yeast nutrient
A Port, Bordeaux or Burgundy yeast (whichever character wine
you may desire)

Method:

Place the elderberries, chopped raisins, and sugar in a polythene bucket. Pour on 4.5 litres (1 gal.) of *boiling* water. Allow to cool 20°C (70°C), add the yeast, nutrient and citric acid. Allow to ferment for one week. Strain into a demijohn with fermentation lock. Fermentation will be complete in 6–7 weeks. Rack into bottles and stopper lightly with cotton wool for 2–3 weeks. Then cork. This is one of the finest red wines that the amateur winemaker can make and compares most favourably with good claret. For other wines the elderberries can be replaced with bilberries, rowan berries, or sloes, all of which will give excellent results.

Elderberry Enchant

Ingredients:

1.3 kg (3 lb.) elderberries (or 335 g (¾ lb.) dried elderberries)
850 ml (1½ pts.) grape juice concentrate (or 1.8 kg (4 lb.) or more
fresh grapes)
450 g (1 lb.) cornflour (also known as yellow cornmeal)
1 kg (2¼ lb.) sugar (or 1.3 kg (3 lb.) honey)
55 g (2 oz.) crushed barley (wheat or wholemeal rice)
280 ml (½ pt.) strong tea
15 g (½ oz.) tartaric acid
15 g (½ oz.) citric acid
15 g (¼ oz.   10 g ammonium phosphate
Water to finally make up 4.5 litres (1 gal.) of "must"
Yeast nutrient and activated wine yeast

Method:

Place the berries, cornflower, sugar and grains into the initial fermentation vessel. Pour in the *boiling* water, macerate the fruits and stir well with a wooden spoon to break up the berries and dissolve the sugar. When cool, add the grape concentrate, tartaric and citric acid, tea, ammonium phosphate, and yeast nutrient. Introduce the activated wine yeast and ferment "on the pulp" for 7 days, stirring the "must" daily with a wooden spoon and keeping closely covered. Then strain, for secondary fermentation, into fermentation vessel and fit air-lock. Leave to ferment in the normal way, racking as necessary.

Elderberry and Apricot (dry, red)

Ingredients:

900 g (2 lb.) elderberries
450 g (1 lb.) dried apricots or peaches (900 g (2 lb.) may be used if desired)
110 g (4 oz.) dried bananas (or 900 g (2 lb.) fresh bananas)
450 g (1 lb.) raisins or sultanas (or 280 ml (½ pt.) white grape concentrate may be used instead)
15 g (½ oz.) tartaric/citric acid mixed, i.e. 7.5 g (¼ oz.) each
30 g (1 oz.) glycerine (B.P. quality)
1.3 kg (3 lb.)sugar
Yeast nutrient and activated (Pommard) wine yeast
Sufficient water to finally produce 4.5 litres (1 gal.) of "must"

Method:

Strip the elderberries and place them and the other fruit with the sugar in the initial fermentation vessel. Pour in *boiling* water and stir to dissolve the sugar. When cool add the strong tea acids, glycerine, yeast nutrient and introduce the activated yeast. Cover well, and leave to ferment for 7 days, then strain into fermentation bottles and fit air lock. Leave to ferment in the normal way, racking later as necessary.

Elderberry and Beetroot
(med. sweet)

Ingredients:

1.3 kg (3 lb.) elderberries (or 335 g (¾ lb.) dried elderberries)
900 g (2 lb.) beetroot (or sugar beet)
450 g (1 lb.) raisins
   (or 450 g (1 lb.) figs, dates, sultanas, currants, etc.)
55 g (2 oz.) dried bananas
   (or 450 g (1 lb.) bananas including skins)
1.3 kg (3 lb.) sugar (or 1.8 kg (4 lb.) honey)
15 g (½ oz.) citric acid (or 3 lemons, no pith, in lieu)
280 ml (½ pt.) strong tea (or a pinch of grape tannin)
Pectic enzyme
Water to finally make up 4.5 litres (1 gal.) of "must"
Yeast nutrient and activated wine yeast

Method:

Wash the beetroot, do not peel, slice up thinly and boil in water until tender, but not mushy. Place the elderberries and chopped dried fruits together with the sugar into the initial fermentation vessel and strain on to these the *boiling* beetroot liquor. Stir well with a wooden spoon to break up the berries and to dissolve the sugar. When cool add the citric acid, strong tea, pectinol and yeast nutrient. Introduce the activated wine yeast and ferment "on the pulp" for 7 days, stirring the "must" daily with a wooden spoon. Then strain for secondary fermentation, into fermentation vessel and fit air-lock. Leave to ferment in the normal way, racking as necessary.

Elderberry and Carrot (dry, red)

Ingredients:

900 g (2 lb.) elderberries
900 g (2 lb.) carrots
450 g (1 lb.) malt extract
900 g (2 lb.) sugar
1 level teaspoon citric acid
Water to finally make up 4.5 litres (1 gal.) of "must"
Yeast nutrient and activated wine yeast

Method:

Scrub and thinly slice the carrots and place these in a sauce pan containing *boiling* water and simmer for 10 minutes, then place the berries, malt extract and sugar into the initial fermentation vessel and pour over these the carrots and *boiling* carrot liquor. Stir well with a wooden spoon to break up the berries and to dissolve the malt extract and sugar. When cool, add the acid and yeast nutrient. Introduce the activated wine yeast and ferment "on the pulp" for 7 days, stirring the "must" daily with a wooden spoon. Then strain, for secondary fermentation, into fermentation vessel and fit air-lock. Leave to ferment in the normal way, racking as necessary.

Elderberry and Red Gooseberry

Ingredients:

900 g (2 lb.) elderberries (or 225 g (½ lb.) dried elderberries)
450 g (1 lb.) red gooseberries (or blackberries/loganberries, etc.)
450 g (1 lb.) raisins (or mixed dried fruit, currants, sultanas, etc.)
1.3 kg (3 lb.) sugar (or 1.8 kg (4 lb.) honey)
1 level teaspoon citric acid (or 3 lemons, no pith, in lieu)
Pectic enzyme
Water to finally make up 4.5 litres (1 gal.) of "must"
Yeast nutrient and activated wine yeast

Method:

Macerate the fruits and place these together with the chopped dried fruits and sugar into the initial fermentation vessel. Pour in the *boiling* water and stir well with a wooden spoon to dissolve the sugar. When cool, add the acid, pectinol and yeast nutrient. Introduce the activated wine yeast and ferment on the "pulp" for 7 days, stirring the must twice daily with a wooden spoon and keep closely covered. Then strain, for secondary fermentation, into fermentation vessel and fit air-lock. Leave to ferment in the normal way, racking as necessary.

Elderberry and Hawthornberry (medium)

Ingredients.

   1.3 kg (3 lb.) elderberries (or 335 g (¾ lb.) dried elderberries)
   900 g (2 lb.) hawthornberries
      (or 225 g (½ lb.) dried bilberries or rowanberries)
   450 g (1 lb.) wholemeal rice (crushed maize, barley or wheat may be substituted)
   450 g (1 lb.) raisins (or sultanas, figs, currants, etc.)
   1.3 kg (3 lb.) sugar (or 1.8 kg (4 lb.) honey)
   15 g (½ oz.) citric acid (or 3 lemons, no pith, in lieu)
   280 ml (½ pt.) strong tea (or a pinch of grape tannin)
   pectin enzyme
   Water to finally make up (4.5 litres (1 gal.) of "must"
   Yeast nutrient and activated wine yeast

Method:

Place the berries, grains, chopped dried fruits, and sugar into the initial fermentation vessel. Pour in the *boiling* water. Macerate the fruits and stir well with a wooden spoon to break up the fruits and dissolve the sugar. When cool add the acid, strong tea, pectinol and yeast nutrient. Introduce the activated wine yeast and ferment on the "pulp" for 7 days, stirring the "must" daily with a wooden spoon and keep closely covered. Then strain for secondary fermentation, into fermentation vessel and fit air-lock. Leave to ferment in the normal way, racking as necessary.

3 lb Elderberries   1/2 oz citric
1 lb Raisin   Yeast + Nutrient
3 lb Sugar   4.5 litres Water

4.5 litres (1 gal) to boil

Crush elder + add chopped raisins

add boiled water.

Cool water to 20°C — add
    yeast and nutrient

Cover + leave 3 days stirring
daily

Strain + add sugar

transfer to demijohn + cover
    with cloth.

Elderberry and Huckleberry (sweet)

Ingredients:

900 g (2 lb.) elderberries
*900 g (2 lb.) huckleberries
55 g (2 oz.) dried bananas
1.3 kg (3 lb.) sugar
1 level teaspoon citric acid
Pectic enzyme
Water to finally make up 4.5 litres (1 gal.) of "must"
Yeast nutrient and activated wine yeast
  *Only the garden huckleberry, *Solanum Nigrum* var. *Guinense* should be used – other varieties may prove inedible.

Method:

Place the berries and dried fruit into the initial fermentation vessel. Pour in the *boiling* water. Macerate the fruits and stir well with a wooden spoon to break up the berries and dissolve the sugar. When cool, add the acid, pectinol and yeast nutrient. Introduce the activated wine yeast and ferment "on the pulp" for 10 days, stirring the "must" twice daily with a wooden spoon and keep closely covered. Then strain, for secondary fermentation, into fermentation vessel and fit air-lock. Leave to ferment in the normal way, racking as necessary.

Elderberry and Marrow

Ingredients:

1.3 kg (3 lb.) elderberries (or 335 g (¾ lb.) dried elderberries)
2.25 kg (5 lb.) ripe marrow (or melon)
450 g (1 lb.) malt extract
1.3 kg (3 lb.) sugar (or 1.8 kg (4 lb.) honey)
15 g citric acid (or 3 lemons, no pith, in lieu)
280 ml (½ pt.) strong tea (or a pinch of grape tannin)
Pectic enzyme
Water to finally make up 4.5 litres (1 gal.) of "must"
Yeast nutrient and activated wine yeast

Method:

Place the berries and shredded marrow (including skin and seeds) together with the malt extract and sugar into the initial fermentation vessel. Pour in the *boiling* water. Macerate the fruits and stir well with a wooden spoon to break up the fruits and to dissolve the sugar. When cool, add the citric acid, strong tea, pectic enzyme, and yeast nutrient. Introduce the activated wine yeast and ferment on the "pulp" for 7 days, stirring the "must" daily with a wooden spoon, and keep closely covered. Then strain, for secondary fermentation, into fermentation vessel and fit air-lock. Leave to ferment in the normal way, racking as necessary.

Elderberry and Pear

Ingredients:

    1.3 kg (3 lb.) elderberries (or 335 g (¾ lb.) dried elderberries)
    1.3 kg (3 lb.) ripe pears (or 1.3 kg (3 lb.) mixed apples or 450 g
       (1 lb.) dried apples/pears)
    450 g (1 lb.) raisins (or mixed dried fruit, currants, sultanas, etc.)
    1.3 kg (3 lb.) sugar (or 1.8 kg (4 lb.) honey)
    10 g (¼ oz.) citric acid (or 3 lemons, no pith, in lieu)
    140 ml (¼ pt.) strong tea (or a pinch of grape tannin)
    Pectic enzyme
    Water to finally make up 4.5 litres (1 gal.) of "must"
    Yeast nutrient and activated wine yeast

Method:

Place the elderberries, shredded pears, dried fruit and sugar into the initial fermentation vessel. Pour in the *boiling* water, and stir well with a wooden spoon to break up the fruits and to dissolve the sugar. When cool, add the citric acid, strong tea, pectinol and yeast nutrient. Introduce the activated wine yeast and ferment on the "pulp" for 7 days, stirring the "must" daily with a wooden spoon and keep closely covered. Then strain, for secondary fermentation, into fermentation vessel, and fit air-lock. Leave to ferment in the normal way, racking and topping up as necessary.

Elderflower and Apricot

Ingredients:

280 ml (½ pt.) elderflowers (or a 55 g (2 oz.) packet of dried
  flowers)
450 g (1 lb.) dried apricots or peaches (900 g (2 lb.) may be used
  if desired)
110 g (4 oz.) dried bananas (or 900 g (2 lb.) fresh bananas)
450 g (1 lb.) raisins or sultanas (or 280 ml (½ pt.) white grape
  concentrate may be used instead)
280 ml (½ pt.) strong tea (or ¼ teaspoonful grape tannin)
15 g (½ oz.) tartaric/citric acid mixed, i.e., 10 g (¼ oz.) each
30 g (1 oz.) glycerine (B.P. quality)
1.3 kg (3 lb.) sugar
Yeast nutrient and activated (Sauternes) wine yeast sufficient to
  finally produce 4.5 litres (1 gal.) of "must"

Method:

Prepare the flower heads, chop the fruits and place these
together with the sugar into the initial fermentation vessel. Pour in
boiling water and stir to dissolve the sugar. When cool add the
strong tea, acids, glycerine, yeast nutrient and introduce the
activated yeast. Cover well, and leave to ferment for 7 days, then
siphon into fermentation bottles and fit air-lock. Leave to ferment
in the normal way, racking later as necessary in due course. The
flower heads should be gathered on a fine day and use only those in
full bloom. If dried elderflower and dried fruits are used,
elderflower wine can be made all the year round.

Elderflower and Carrot

Ingredients:

280 ml (½ pt.) elderflowers (or a 55 g (2 oz.) packet of dried
   flowers)
1.3 kg (3 lb.) young carrots
450 g (1 lb.) raisins/sultanas or figs
15 g (½ oz.) citric acid (or 3 lemons, no pith, in lieu)
280 ml (½ pt.) strong tea (or ¼ teaspoonful grape tannin)
1.3 kg (3 lb.) sugar
Yeast nutrient and activated wine yeast
Sufficient water to finally produce 4.5 litres (1 gal.) of "must"

Method:

Scrub the young carrots and slice thinly. Boil the carrots until
they are *just tender*. Place the prepared flowers, chopped fruit, and
sugar into the initial fermentation vessel and strain over these, the
boiling carrot extract. Stir well to dissolve the sugar. When cool
add the acid, strong tea, yeast nutrient and introduce the activated
wine yeast. Cover well and leave to ferment for 7 days. Then siphon
into fermentation bottles and fit air-lock. Leave to ferment in
normal way, racking later as necessary. The delicate, fragrant and
wholly delectable elderflower wine can only be produced by using
flower heads of full bloom, otherwise a bitter taste may be
imparted to the wine.

Elderflower and Cider

Ingredients:

280 ml (½ pt.) elderflowers (or a 55 g (2 oz.) packet of dried
   flowers)
1 litre (1 qt.) bottle commercial, draught or home-made cider
450 g (1 lb.) raisins or sultanas
15 g (½ oz.) citric acid (or 3 lemons, no pith, in lieu)
140 ml (¼ pt.) strong tea (or ¼ teaspoonful grape tannin)
1.3 kg (3 lb.) sugar
Yeast nutrient and activated wine yeast
Sufficient water to finally produce 4.5 litres (1 gal.) "must"

Method:

Prepare the elderflowers and place these with the chopped fruit and sugar in the initial fermentation vessel and pour over the *boiling* water and stir well to dissolve the sugar. When cool add the juice of the lemons, strong tea and yeast nutrient, and introduce the activated wine yeast. Cover well and leave to ferment for 7 days. Then siphon into fermentation bottles and add the cider. Fit air-lock and ferment in normal way, racking as necessary in due course. This wine, if using dried material, can be made at any time of the year. Remember to use only just sufficient elderflowers.

Elderflower and Honey

Ingredients:

380 ml (²/₃ pt.) elderflower (or a 55 g (2 oz.) packet of dried flowers)
Honey – mild, clover, lime, heather, Empire – any kind will do
1.3 kg (3 lb.) – dry recipe
2.6 kg (6 lb.) – sweet recipe
15 g (½ oz.) citric acid (or 3 lemons, no pith, in lieu)
280 ml (½ pt.) strong tea (or ¼ teaspoonful grape tannin)
Yeast nutrient and activated (Maury) wine yeast
Sufficient water to finally produce 4.5 litres (1 gal.) "must"

Method:

Prepare the flower heads and place them in the initial fermentation vessel and pour over the flowers the *boiling* water. Then stir in the honey until dissolved. Sugar in proportion 450 g to 675 g (1 lb. to 1½ lb.) honey may be partly or wholly substituted. If the sweet recipe is followed add the honey in several stages to avoid a "sticking" fermentation. When cool add the acid, strong tea, yeast nutrient and introduce the activated wine yeast, an extra 10 g (¼ oz.) of acid and half as much again yeast nutrient may be used in this recipe if desired. Cover well and ferment for 7 days. Then siphon into fermentation bottles and fit air-lock. Leave to ferment in normal way, racking later as necessary. Never exceed (1.2–1.5 litres) (2–3 pts.) florets; in most cases 280 ml (½ pt.) is sufficient, otherwise the delightful fragrance will be excessive.

Elderflower and Oak Leaf

Ingredients:

280 ml (½ pt.) elderflowers (or a 55 g (2 oz.) packet of dried flowers)
2.25 litres (½ gal.) young oak leaves (or bramble tips)
110 g (4 oz.) dried bananas (or 570 ml (1 pt.) crushed barley)
450 g (1 lb.) raisins, sultanas or figs, etc.
1 level teaspoon citric acid (or 2 lemons, no pith, in lieu)
280 ml (½ pt.) strong tea (or ¼ teaspoonful grape tannin)
1.3 kg (3 lb.) sugar
Yeast nutrient and activated wine yeast
Sufficient water to finally produce 4.5 litre "must"

Method:

Wash the oak leaves or tips, then place these in a boiler and bring to *boiling* point; cut off the heat and leave to infuse (as in tea making) for 1 hour. Place the prepared elderflowers, chopped fruits, and grains if used, together with the sugar into the initial fermentation vessel. Bring the oak leaves back to *boiling* point only and strain the extract into the initial fermentation vessel. Stir well to dissolve the sugar. When cool add the acid, strong tea, yeast nutrient, and introduce the activated wine yeast. Cover well and leave to ferment 7 days, then strain into fermentation bottles and fit air-lock, racking as necessary.

Elderflower and Rhubarb

Ingredients:

280 ml (½ pt.) elderflowers (or a 55 g (2 oz.) packet of dried flowers)
1.3 kg (3 lb.) rhubarb (gooseberries or gooseberries and rhubarb may be used)
450 g (1 lb.) raisins or sultanas 280 ml (½ pt.) of white grape concentrate or 110 g (4 oz.) dried bananas may be substituted)
15 g (½ oz.) citric acid (or 3 lemons, no pith, in lieu)
280 ml strong tea (or ¼ teaspoonful grape tannin)
1.3 kg (3 lb.) sugar
Yeast nutrient and activated wine yeast
Sufficient water to finally product 4.5 litres (1 gal.) "must"

Method:

Clean and slice the rhubarb and soak in *cold* water for 48 hours. Remember to add one Campden tablet and keep closely covered. Then prepare the elderflowers, being sure not to use any green stalks, and place these in the initial fermentation vessel together with the chopped fruits and sugar. Pour over this the *boiling* water and stir to dissolve the sugar. When cool add the rhubarb and rhubarb juice, grape concentrate if used, acid and strong tea and yeast nutrient and introduce the activated wine yeast. Closely cover and leave to ferment for 7 days. Then siphon into fermentation bottles and fit air-lock. Leave to ferment in normal way, racking as necessary.

Elderflower and Rosehip

Ingredients:

280 ml (½ pt.) elderflowers (or a 55 g (2 oz.) packet of dried flowers)
110 g (¼ lb.) dried rose-hips (or 110 g (4 oz.) rose-hip/shells)
450 g (1 lb.) raisins, sultanas or dried apricots, etc.
15 g (½ oz.) citric acid (or 3 lemons, no pith, in lieu)
280 ml (½ pt.) strong tea (or ¼ teaspoonful grape tannin)
1.3 kg (3 lb.) sugar
Yeast nutrient and activated wine yeast
Sufficient water to finally produce 4.5 litres (1 gal.) of "must"

Method:

Prepare the flowers and place these into the initial fermentation vessel together with the sugar and chopped fruits. Pour in the *boiling* water to dissolve the sugar and stir well. When cool add the acid, strong tea, yeast nutrient and introduce the activated wine yeast. Cover well and ferment for 10 days, then siphon into fermentation bottles and fit air lock. Leave to ferment in normal way, racking as necessary in due course. A strong, medium-sweet "social" wine with an attractive bouquet and light tawny colour.

Fig and Grape Concentrate

Ingredients:

450 g (1 lb.) dried figs
570 ml (1 pt.) grape concentrate (white or red)
110 g (4 oz.) dried bananas (or 85 g (3 oz.) dried rose-hips/shells)
1 kg (2¼ lb.) sugar
10 g (¼ oz.) citric acid
140 ml (¼ pt.) strong tea
Yeast nutrient and activated wine yeast
Water, sufficient to finally produce 4.5 litres (1 gal.) of "must"

Method:

Place the chopped fruits into the initial fermentation vessel, add the sugar, and pour in four pints of *boiling* water. Stir well with a wooden spoon to dissolve the sugar, etc. When cool (20°C)(70°F) add the citric acid, strong tea, yeast nutrient and add the grape concentrate which has been dissolved in the remainder of the warm water (*not boiling*). Be sure the "must" is not over (20°C)(70°F) and introduce the activated wine yeast. Cover securely and leave to ferment 7 days, then strain into secondary fermentation vessels. Fit air-lock and leave to ferment in the normal way, racking as necessary.

Variation:

1. A 900 g (2 lb.) tin of Australian grape jam may be used in lieu of the grape concentrate.

2. 225 g (½ lb.) malt extract may be added or used in lieu of bananas.

"Have you got a drop of vinegar I could have?"

Flower Wines

The most popular flower wines are, nowadays, dandelion, broom, and coltsfoot (the last being as a rule more difficult to track down). They all make delicate, light and attractive wines which are pleasant in themselves and invaluable for blending with other wines which may be lacking bouquet.

We can no longer recommend you to make primrose or cowslip wine, as in the old days, owing to the increasing scarcity of these flowers, which now need protection.

Ingredients:

4.5 litres (1 gal.) flowers – gorse, broom, coltsfoot
1 orange, 1 lemon
1.5 kg (3½ lb.) sugar
Yeast and nutrient

These flower wines seem to be best made as sweet wines, and 1.5 kg (3½ lb.) sugar will give this result, but the broom wine is also agreeable when made dry, with 1.3 kg (3 lb.) or even only 1.1 kg (2½ lb.) of sugar to 4.5 litres (1 gal.).

Method:

Bring the water to the boil and stir into it the sugar, making sure that it is all dissolved. Put the peel of the orange and lemon into a crock, bowl, or polythene bucket, being careful to exclude all white pith, to prevent the wine from having a bitter taste, and pour the hot syrup over the rinds. Allow to cool (20°C)(70°F), then add the flowers, the juice of the fruit, your chosen yeast, and some yeast nutrient. Cover closely and leave for five days in a warm place, stirring each day. Then strain through a nylon sieve into a fermenting jar, filling it to the bottom of the neck, and fit a fermentation trap. Leave for three months, then siphon the wine off the yeast deposit into a fresh jar. A further racking after another three months is helpful, and shortly after that the wine will be fit to drink, if still young.

Ginger (1)

Ingredients:

30 g (1 oz.) essence of ginger
15 g (½ oz.) yeast
Water: 4.5 litres (1 gal.)

900 g (2 lb.) granulated sugar
15 g (½ oz.) tartaric acid
15 g (½ oz.) cream of tartar

Method:

Mix sugar, tartaric acid, and cream of tartar. Dissolve in 4.5 litres (1 gal.) of very hot water. Make up to 12 litres(10 qts.) adding cold/warm water so that your liquid is at about 20°C (70°F). Cream the yeast with some of the liquid and add to the bulk. Add the ginger essence and stir well. Bottle in screw stopper bottles and store at about 12–15°C (50–60°F). Note: screw down stoppers tightly.

After three days, put quarter Campden tablet into each bottle. Screw down tightly again and you may drink on the fifth day. If you do not use Campden tablets you will risk bursting bottles.

The cost works out less than 5p a bottle, is foolproof and is far superior to that you can buy.

Ginger (2)

Ingredients:

30 g (1 oz.) bruised root ginger
280 ml (½ pt.) strong tea
10 g (¼ oz.) citric acid (or 2 lemons, no pith, in lieu)
1 kg (2¼ lb.) sugar
Yeast nutrient and yeast (activated)
Water, sufficient to produce 4.5 litres (1 gal.) of "must"

Method:

Crush the ginger and place this in the initial fermentation vessel, add the sugar and pour in the *boiling* water. Stir to dissolve the sugar. When cool (20°C)(70°F) add the citric acid, strong tea, yeast nutrient and activated yeast. Ferment for 7 days then strain into fermentation bottle. Fit air-lock and ferment in normal way, racking as necessary. *The cheapest of all wines!*

Ginger (3)

(Resulting quantity about 14 litres) (26 pints)

Ingredients:

2.25 litres (½ gal.) white concentrated grape juice of S.G. 1.385
165 g (6 oz.) of bruised ginger
55 g (2 oz.) of tartaric acid
1.8 kg (4 lb.) sugar and 450 g (1 lb.) of glucose
15 g (½ oz.) of candied angelica (grated)

Method:

Part "A": Mix 2.25 litres (½ gal.) white concentrated grape juice with 6.75 litres (1½ gal.) of water.

Part "B": Mix 4.5 litres (1 gal.) with 1.8 kg (4 lb.) of sugar; 55 g (2 oz.) tartaric acid and 165 g (6 oz.) of bruised ginger and the 15 g (2 oz.) of angelica.

Boil ingredients of Part "B" for about 10 minutes (simmer) leave to cool, and then mix with mixture of Part "A". Add the wine culture (yeast) and leave to ferment for about 30 days when the wine should be decanted and seven days after decanted again. The wine is then ready for tasting; a rich wine.

The 450 g (1 lb.) of glucose can be added to the brew, during the fermentation process in small portions.

The alcohol content of this wine is high.

Gooseberry (dry white)

Ingredients:

1.8 kg (4 lb.) gooseberries	1.3 kg (3 lb.) sugar
Water to 4.5 litres (1 gal.)	Yeast and nutrient

Method:

Wash gooseberries. Crush them in jar. Pour on 4.5 litres (1 gal.) *boiling* water. Cover closely and leave for 10 days. Strain off liquid and bring to boil and pour over the sugar. Stir a few seconds, leave till cool (20°C) (70°F), and add yeast and nutrient. Cover tightly again. Stir daily for seven days. Strain into fermenting jar. Fit air-lock, racking as necessary.

Gooseberry and Grape

Ingredients:

1.8 kg (4 lb.) green or red gooseberries
570 ml (1 pt.) grape concentrate (white or red)
1.3 kg (3 lb.) sugar
55 g (2 oz.) dried bananas or 85 g (3 oz.) dried rose-hips/shells
20 g (¾ oz.) glycerine (B.P. quality)
15 g (½ oz.) citric acid (or 3 lemons, no pith, in lieu)
280 ml (½ pt.) strong tea (or grape tannin)
Yeast nutrient and activated wine yeast
Water; sufficient to finally produce 4.5 litres (1 gal.) "must"

Method:

Wash, then top and tail the gooseberries. Ensure that there are no lower heads or stalks left amongst the fruit, as their inclusion will give an undesirable flavour. The gooseberry does not lend itself to pressing, therefore break open the fruits and always ferment "on the pulp". Place the prepared fruit into the initial fermentation vessel, together with the dried fruit and sugar and pour in the *boiling* water, stirring well to dissolve the sugar. When cool add the citric acid, strong tea, yeast nutrient and introduce the activated wine yeast. Cover well and leave to ferment on the pulp seven days, then strain into fermentation bottles – avoid pressing the fruit. At this stage add the grape concentrate and glycerine. Fit air-lock and leave to ferment in the normal way, racking later as necessary.

As a variation:

140 ml (¼ pt.) (or ½ packet dried) elderflowers can be introduced in the initial stage of fermentation.

Grapefruit

Ingredients:

6 sweet grapefruit
1 kg (2¼ lb.) white sugar
Yeast and nutrient

Pectic enzyme
Water to make up 4.5 litres
   (1 gal.)

Method:

Put the thin peel from one of the fruits into a bowl, add the juice of all six and 3.5 litres (6 pts.) of water, the yeast nutrient, the crushed Campden tablet and the pectin destroying enzyme (e.g., Pektolase or Pectinol). Leave covered. The next day add the yeast and sugar; stir thoroughly until it is all dissolved. Leave two days, still covered, then strain into fermenting jar, make up to 4.5 litre with cold, boiled water and fit trap. Ferment out, and rack and bottle when completely clear.

Huckleberry and Rowanberry

Ingredients:

1.3 kg (3 lb.) huckleberries (or 335 g (¾ lb.) dried bilberries)
900 g (2 lb.) rowanberries (or hawthorn berries)
450 g (1 lb.)raisins (or sultanas, dates, figs, etc.)
1.3 kg (3 lb.)sugar (or 1.8kg (4 lb.) honey)
15 g (½ oz.) citric acid (or 3 lemons, no pith, in lieu)
280 ml (½ pt.) strong tea (or a pinch of grape tannin)
Pectic enzyme
Water to finally make up 4.5 litres (1 gal.) of "must"
Yeast nutrient and activated wine yeast

Method:

Place the berries and chopped dried fruits together with the sugar into the initial fermentation vessel (only use the garden huckleberry variety *Solanum Nigrum var. Guinense* – other varieties may prove inedible). Pour on the *boiling* water. Macerate the fruits and stir well with a wooden spoon to break up the berries and dissolve the sugar. When cool, add the citric acid, strong tea, pectinol and yeast nutrient. Introduce the activated wine yeast and ferment on the pulp for 7 days, stirring the must daily with a wooden spoon and keep closely covered. Then strain, for secondary fermentation, into fermentation vessel and fit air-lock. Leave to ferment in the normal way, racking as necessary.

Lemon and Apricot

Ingredients:

½ bottle pure lemon juice (such as "P.L.J.")
450 g (1 lb.) dried apricots (or figs)
1.3 kg (3 lb.) sugar (or 1.8 kg (4 lb.) invert sugar)
Yeast nutrient and activated wine yeast
Water; sufficient to finally produce 4.5 litres (1 gal.) of "must"

Method:

Place the chopped apricots and sugar into the initial fermentation vessel. Pour in the hot water and stir well to dissolve the sugar. When cool (20°C)(70°F) add the lemon juice and yeast nutrient. Introduce the activated wine yeast. Cover securely and leave to ferment for 7 days on the pulp, stirring occasionally. Then strain into the secondary fermentation vessel and fit air-lock. Leave to ferment in the normal way and rack later as necessary.

Variations:

1. Add 225 g (½ lb.)chopped raisins if you wish.
2. Add 335 g (¾ lb.) crushed barley, wheat, or maize.

N.B. The lemon juice may be heavily sulphited, therefore be sure the yeast is well activated and it is desirable to add the lemon juice in stages over three days to avoid a "sticking" of the fermentation.

Lemon Thyme

This herb grows profusely in many gardens, and in late May a most pleasant wine can be made from its leaves. This recipe will produce a light and fragrant table wine not unlike a Moselle.

Ingredients:

570 ml (1 pt.) lemon thyme leaves (no stalks)
900 g (2 lb.) raisins   Water to 4.5 litres (1 gal.)
1 kg sugar (2¼ lb.)   Yeast and nutrient

Method:

Chop the lemon thyme (to approximately the size of mint when making mint sauce). Pour *boiling* water over it, then add the raisins. Keep closely covered, but stir every day for 7 days. Strain on to the sugar, stir thoroughly and add yeast, wine yeast, or a level teaspoonful of granulated yeast. Leave to ferment, closely covered and in a warm place, for another two weeks. Strain into fermenting vessel and fit air lock, and leave until it has fermented right out. Ladies may prefer to add 225–450 g (½ lb.–1 lb.) sugar to obtain a much sweeter wine but this is best added finally, to taste, and not at the outset.

Lime Juice and Raisin

Ingredients:

1 bottle pure lime juice (Rose's)
450 g (1 lb.) raisins (or sultanas)
1.3 kg (3 lb.) sugar (or 1.8 kg (4 lb.) honey)
Yeast nutrient and activated wine yeast
Water; sufficient to finally produce 4.5 litres (1 gal.) of "must"

Method:

Place the sugar and chopped raisins into the initial fermentation vessel. Pour in the hot water and stir well to dissolve the sugar.

When cool (20°C, 70°F) add the lime juice and yeast nutrient. Introduce the activated wine yeast. Cover securely and leave to ferment for 7 days on the "pulp", stirring occasionally. Then strain into the secondary fermentation vessel, top up, and fit air-lock. Leave to ferment in the normal way and rack as necessary.

Variations:
1. Use 570 ml (1 pt.) of grape concentrate in lieu of raisins.
2. Add 55 g (2 oz.) dried rose-hips/shells if you wish or 55 g (2 oz.) dried bananas.

N.B. To avoid a "sticking" of the fermentation, be most sure to add a well activated yeast, and add the lime juice preferably in stages over three days due to the lime juice being heavily sulphited. This will dissipate on refermentation.

Liqueurs

Most of the following can be made in 1 litre screw top jar or a 2 lb Kilner jar, or slightly larger receptacle in the case of large fruit.

ADVOCAAT
This has a pleasant flavour that disguises its potency; but potent it is. Make it 9 to 10 days before serving, depending upon the weather. It "comes" more quickly in hot weather.

Ingredients:

3 eggs	**165 g (6 oz.) sugar**
3 juicy lemons	**165 g (6 oz.) milk**
Bottled pure lemon juice	**165 g (6 oz.) rum**

Method:
Put the eggs (raw and in their shells) into a bowl just big enough for all three to rest on the bottom. Squeeze over them juice from the lemons, adding enough bottled juice to submerge them. If the

eggs float, put a cap of half a squeezed lemon on each. Cover the bowl with muslin and leave in a cool place for 8–9 days, until the egg shells dissolve, or nearly so. Then strain and squeeze (shells and all) through muslin. Beat. Add sugar. Beat. Add milk. Beat. Add rum. Beat. Bottle. Put on ice for 24 hours before serving, as a before dinner aperitif.

APRICOT BRANDY

Approximately 20 apricots
225 g (½ lb.) of sugar
3–400 ml (½–¾ pt.) of brandy

ATHOL BROSE

This is served as a before-dinner aperitif, and should be made five days before the party. It does not keep indefinitely. And beware! It slips down so easily that your guests may not realise its potency.

Ingredients:

3 heaped dessertspoons Quaker oats (not the "instant" kind)	**250 ml (8 oz.) whisky**
	3 dessertspoons sherry
225 g (8 oz.) cream	**2 dessertspoons liquid honey**

Method:

Soak the Quaker oats in water to cover. Next morning strain through muslin into a large jug. The resultant liquid is called brae. To this add cream. Stir. Add whisky. Stir. Add sherry. Stir. Add honey. Stir very thoroughly, for the honey is apt to sink to the bottom. Bottle the mixture and keep in the refrigerator until an hour or so before your guests are expected. Take it out, let it thaw a little, stir well, and pour into a bowl, ready to ladle out (stirring again) into sherry glasses.

BLACKBERRY BRANDY (See Cassis)

CASSIS (same proportions for Blackberry Liqueur)

¾ fill jar with crushed blackcurrants
165 g (6 oz.) sugar per 570 ml (1 pt.) capacity
Top up with gin or other spirit

CHERRY BRANDY

450 g (1 lb.) Morello cherries
225 g (½ lb.) caster sugar
12 almonds
Top up with brandy

CREME DE MENTHE

Sounds expensive when you learn that the base is two bottles of gin. But when you realise that this makes nearly three bottles of liqueur, of which far less is consumed per person than when gin is drunk in the usual ways, and, moreover, that you only drink it on occasion, and that it keeps indefinitely, you may revise your opinion.

N.B. Before producing it at the dinner table, make sure to loosen the cork or stopper of bottle or decanter. The sugar content is apt to make it stick.

Required:

**3 empty gin (or other)
   bottles**
**1 kg (2 lb. 4 oz.) granulated
   sugar**

2 bottles gin
Peppermint essence
Green colouring

Method:

Into each bottle pour 335 g (12 oz.) sugar, then fill with gin to within 2.5 cm (1 in.) of neck. Cork. Several times a day (i.e., whenever you pass the bottles) shake, and in four or five days, when the liquid is quite clear add (to taste) about two teaspoons peppermint essence and about the same of green colouring. Shake once or twice to spread flavour and colour, then cork again and set aside. Mark the date on the bottle and try to give it three months to mature.

DAMSON GIN

    450 g (1 lb.) damsons (pricked)
    165 g (6 oz.) sugar
    Top up with gin

And this damson gin recipe is highly recommended by Mr William A. Walker, of 601 South Red Bank Road, Evansville, Indiana 47712.

Ingredients:

    1.3 kg (3 lb.) damsons   **1 litre (1 qt.) dry gin**
    1.3 kg (3 lb.) sugar

Method:

Puncture each damson five or six times with a fork and drop into a screw cap jar. Add 1.3 kg (3 lb.) sugar and 1 litre (1 qt.) gin. Lay the jar on its side as far as possible and each day rotate half turn. Do not shake. When most of the sugar has dissolved the damson gin is ready for use. Believe you me this is a drink fit for Jupiter! Use sparingly.

FRAMBOISE

    450 g (1 lb.) raspberries
    335 g (¾ lb.) caster sugar
    Spirit

MULBERRY LIQUEUR

    570 ml (1 pt.) of sound mulberries
    140–165 g (4–6 oz.) caster sugar
    Top up with brandy or gin

PEACH BRANDY

Half fill jar with halved peaches
110 g (¼ lb.) caster sugar
110 g (¼ lb.) brown sugar
A few kernels from the peach stones. Top up with brandy

PRUNELLE

¾ jar of ripe sound plums
165 g (6 oz.) caster sugar
A few kernels from the plum stones. Top up with spirit

RED-CURRANT LIQUEUR (*see* Blackcurrant Liqueur or Cassis)

SLOE GIN (October or November)

450 g (1 lb.) sloes
100 g (3–4 oz.) caster sugar
Top up with gin
6 blanched almonds or a small eggspoon of almond essence

WHITE-CURRANT LIQUEUR

1 teaspoon of grated lemon rind
675 g (1½ lb.) white-currants
450 g (1 lb.) caster sugar
A few small pieces of lemon rind
A small teaspoon of ginger essence
Top up the jar with whisky

A MINT FAVOURITE

Strip the leaves off a couple of good sprigs of mint and crush them. Put the crushed leaves into a jug and add three tablespoons of caster sugar. Pour in just enough hot water to dissolve the sugar, add a wineglass of liqueur brandy and fill up with iced water.

ANOTHER MINT FAVOURITE

Thoroughly bruise a few sprigs of mint and place in a lager-type glass. Add two or three tablespoons of crushed ice, and fill up with equal quantities of chilled wine and soda water. Most people like this dry, but sweet-tooths will want to add a little sugar.

Loganberry and Beetroot

Ingredients:

   1.3 kg (3 lb.) loganberries (or blackberries)
   900 g (2 lb.) beetroot
   280 ml (1 pt.) commercial or home-made cider
   1.3 kg (3 lb.) sugar
   2 lemons
   Pectic enzyme
   Water to finally make up 4.5 litres (1 gal.) of "must"
   Yeast nutrient and activated wine yeast

Method:

Wash the beetroot (do not peel) and slice into thin rings. Place in a saucepan and simmer in the usual way until tender. Place the berries and sugar into the initial fermentation vessel and strain into this the hot beetroot liquor. Macerate and stir well with a wooden spoon to break up the berries and to dissolve the sugar. When *cool* add the cider or concentrated "must", lemon juice, Pectinol and yeast nutrient. Introduce the activated wine yeast and ferment on the "pulp" for 7 days, stirring the must daily with a wooden spoon, and keep it closely covered. Then strain, for secondary fermentation, into fermentation vessel and fit air-lock. Leave to ferment in the normal way, racking as necessary.

Loganberry and Blackcurrant

Ingredients:

   1.8 kg (4 lb.) loganberries
   900 g (2 lb.) black-currants (or 450 g (1 lb.) red-currants)
   10 g (¼ oz.) citric acid (or 2 lemons, no pith)
   3 g ($^1/_{10}$ oz.) grape tannin (or 280 ml (½ pt.) strong tea)
   1.3 kg (3 lb.) sugar
   Yeast nutrient and activated wine yeast
   Water; sufficient to finally produce 4.5 litres (1 gal.) of "must"

Method:

Place the fruits into the initial fermentation vessel and macerate these with a wooden spoon then pour in the *boiling* water, add the sugar and stir well until dissolved. When cool add the acid, tannin (and 15 g (½ oz.) pectinol if you wish), and yeast nutrient, introduce the activated wine yeast and secure closely, leaving to ferment for five days. Then transfer through nylon strainer into fermentation bottles. Fit air-lock and leave to ferment in normal way, racking, as necessary in due course. A Burgundy yeast is recommended.

Variations:
1. 225 g (½ lb.) malt extract may be added.
2. 20 g (¾ oz.) glycerine may be added at the final fermentation stage, i.e. when fitting the air-lock.

Loganberry and Crab Apple

Ingredients:

1.3 kg (3 lb.) (or more) loganberries (or blackberries)
1.8 kg (4 lb.) crab apples (or mixed apples)
450 g (1 lb.) raisins (dried figs, dates, prunes or apricots, etc.,
    may be substituted)
1.3 kg (3 lb.) sugar
280 ml (½ pt.) strong tea (or pinch of grape tannin)
15 g (½ oz.) citric acid (or 3 lemons, no pith, in lieu)
Pectic enzyme
Water to finally make up to 4.5 litres (1 gal.) of "must"
Yeast nutrient and activated wine yeast

Method:

Wash and cut up the apples into small pieces, skins included, and place these together with the berries, chopped dried fruits and sugar into initial fermentation vessel. Pour in the *boiling* water, macerate and stir well with a wooden spoon to break up the berries and to dissolve the sugar. When cool add the strong tea, citric acid, Pectolase and yeast nutrient. Introduce the activated wine yeast and ferment on the "pulp" for 7 days, stirring the "must" daily with a wooden spoon and keep it closely covered. Then strain, for secondary fermentation, in fermentation vessel and fit air-lock. Leave to ferment in the normal way, racking as necessary.

Loganberry and Plum

Ingredients:

1.3 kg (3 lb.) loganberries (or blackberries)
900 g (2 lb.) plums (or greengages)
110 g (4 oz.) dried bananas (or 900 g (2 lb.) fresh bananas, including skins)
1.3 kg (3 lb.) sugar
2 lemons
Pectic enzyme
Water to make up finally 4.5 litres (1 gal.) of "must"
Yeast nutrient and activated wine yeast

Method:

Place the loganberries into the initial fermentation vessel and add the stoned plums, sugar and either dried bananas or chopped fresh bananas, including skins, then pour on to these the *boiling* water. Mash the fruits with a wooden spoon and stir well to dissolve the sugar. When cool add the lemon juice, Pectolase and yeast nutrient. Introduce the activated wine yeast and ferment on the "pulp" for 7 days, stirring the "must" daily with a wooden spoon and keeping it closely covered, then strain, for secondary fermentation, into fermentation vessel and fit air-lock. Leave to ferment in the normal way, racking as necessary.

Lovage

Ingredients:

    4.5 litres (1 gal.) lovage, florets only
    450 g (1 lb.) malt extract (or 450 g (1 lb.) raisins, etc.)
    1.3 kg (3 lb.) sugar
    280 ml (½ pt.) strong tea (or a pinch of grape tannin)
    15 g (½ oz.) citric acid (or 3 lemons, no pith, in lieu)
    Water to finally make up 4.5 litres (1 gal.) of "must"
    Yeast and activated wine yeast

Method:

Place the florets, malt extract (or chopped fruit) and sugar into the initial fermentation vessel. Pour in the *boiling* water and stir with a wooden spoon to dissolve the sugar and malt extract. When cool add the strong tea, citric acid, and yeast nutrient. Introduce the activated wine yeast and ferment "on the pulp" for 7 days, stirring the "must" daily with a wooden spoon and keep it closely covered. Then strain for secondary fermentation into fermentation vessel and fit air-lock. Leave to ferment in the normal way racking as necessary.

Lovage and Nettle

Ingredients:

    450 g (1 lb.) lovage *(Levisticum Officinale)* florets only
    450 g (1 lb.) nettles
    900 g (2 lb.) bananas including skins (or 110 g (4 oz.) dried bananas)
    450 g (1 lb.) figs (or dates, sultanas, prunes, etc.)
    1.3 kg (3 lb.) sugar
    280 ml (½ pt.) strong tea (or a pinch of grape tannin)
    15 g (½ oz.) citric acid (or 3 lemons, no pith, in lieu)
    Water to finally make up 4.5 litres (1 gal.) "must"
    Yeast nutrient and activated wine yeast

Method:

Shred the lovage leaves and nettles. Place these together with the chopped fruits and sugar into the initial fermentation vessel. Pour in the *boiling* water. Macerate and stir well with a wooden spoon to break up the fruit and to dissolve the sugar. When cool add the citric acid, strong tea and yeast nutrient. Introduce the activated wine yeast and ferment on the "pulp" for 7 days, stirring the "must" daily with a wooden spoon and keep it closely covered. Then strain, for secondary fermentation, into fermentation vessel and fit air-lock. Leave to ferment in the normal way, racking as necessary.

Maize

Ingredients:

570 ml (1 pt.) maize	**2 lemons**
Soak the maize overnight	**1 orange**
900 g (2 lb.) raisins	**1.8 kg (4 lb.) sugar**
Water to 4.5 litres (1 gal.)	
Yeast and yeast nutrient	

Method:

Crush the maize in a mincer and put it into a crock with the chopped raisins, thinly peeled lemon rinds, fruit juice, sugar and yeast nutrient. Pour on the *boiling* water, stir to dissolve sugar, and leave till cool; then add yeast. Keep well covered in a warm place for three weeks, stirring daily, then strain into fermenting bottle and fit trap. Leave to ferment right out and clear, then bottle.

Mangold

Ingredients:

2.7 kg (5 lb.) mangolds	**2 lemons**
Water to 4.5 litres (1 gal.)	**2 oranges**
1.3 kg (3 lb.) sugar (for a medium wine) or	**Yeast nutrient**
1.1 kg (2¼ lb.) sugar (for a dry table wine)	

Method:

Wash the mangolds but do not peel. Cut into pieces and boil until tender. Strain, and add the sugar and the rinds of the oranges and lemons (avoiding the white pith). Boil for 20 minutes. Allow the liquor to cool, and add the juice of the oranges and lemons. Stir in the yeast and leave in a warm place, well covered, for about a week. Then stir before transferring to fermenting jar, and fit air-lock. Leave in a temperature of about 17°C (65°F) until it clears, then rack into clean jar and refit lock. Bottle after a further two months.

Mangold and Caraway

Ingredients:

2.7 kg (5 lb.) mangolds
450 g (1 lb.) chopped raisins (or sultanas, dates, etc)
1.1 kg (2¼ lb.) sugar (or 1.3 kg (3 lb.) honey)
15 g (½ oz.) citric acid (or 3 lemons, no pith)
30 g (1 oz.) caraway seeds
1 tablespoon strong tea
Water to make up finally 4.5 litres (1 gal.) of "must"
Yeast nutrient and activated wine yeast

Method:

Scrub and cut up the beet. Simmer in 4 litres (seven pints) water for 1½ hours, together with the caraway seeds. Pour the beet, seeds and liquor into the initial fermentation vessel in which the chopped fruits and sugar have already been placed. Stir well with a wooden spoon to dissolve the sugar, etc. When cool add the strong tea, citric acid and yeast nutrient. Introduce the activated wine yeast and ferment on the "pulp" for 7 days, stirring the "must" with a wooden spoon, daily, and ensuring that it is closely covered. Then strain, for secondary fermentation, into fermentation vessel and fit air-lock. Leave to ferment in the normal way racking as necessary.

Marigold

Marigolds (Calendula) are grown in nearly every garden from seed, their lovely orange colour adds much gaiety to the garden. Their medicinal properties are well known and wine made from the flower heads possesses many virtues.

Old-time Recipe:

One peck (9 litres) of marigold petals, 675 g (1½ lb.) stoned raisins, 3.1 kg (7 lb.) castor sugar, 900 g (2 lb.) honey, 13.5 litres (3 gals.) water, 3 eggs, 6 oranges, 4 tablespoonsful German yeast, 30 g (1 oz.) gelatine, 450 g (1 lb.) sugar candy, 570 ml (1 pt.) brandy.

Method:

Take a peck (9 litres) of marigold flowers, and put them into an earthenware bowl with the raisins. Pour over them a *boiling* liquid made of the sugar, honey, and 13.5 litres (3 gals.) of water. Clear this liquid while it is *boiling* with the whites and shells of the three eggs and strain it before putting it in the flowers. Cover up the bowl and leave it for two days and nights. Stir it well and leave it for another day and night. Then strain it and put it into a 27 litre (six gallon) cask which has been well cleaned, and add it to 450 g (1 lb.) sugar candy and the rinds of six oranges, which have been peeled and stripped of all white pith. Stir into it four tablespoonsful of German yeast and cover up the bung hole. Leave it to work till it froths out. When the fermentation is over pour in a 570 ml (1 pt.) of brandy and 15 g (½ oz.) dissolved gelatine. Stop the cask and leave it for several months before bottling.

Modern Basic Recipe:

2.25 litres (2 qt.) marigold heads	30 g (1 oz.) citric acid
1.8 kg (4 lb.) sugar	Yeast nutrient
450 g (1 lb.) raisins (chopped)	Yeast culture
Water to 4.5 litres (1 gal.)	1 cup cold tea

Method:

The marigolds should be gathered at the full strength of the midday sun when they are wide open and only the golden petals should be used. Dissolve the sugar in the water, add the chopped raisins and allow to cool. Add the crushed flower heads, citric acid (or lemons and oranges – no pith) and cold tea. When at right temperature add yeast nutrient and yeast culture. Leave for five days, stirring twice daily.

Marrow and Prune

Ingredients:

> 2.7 kg (5 lb.) ripe marrow
> 450 g (1 lb.) prunes (dates, peaches, sultanas, figs, etc., may be used in lieu)
> 55 g (2 oz.) dried rose-hips/shells
> 1.1 kg (2¼ lb.) sugar
> 2 lemons
> Pectic enzyme
> Water to finally make up 4.5 litres (1 gal.) of "must"
> Yeast nutrient and activated wine yeast

Method:

Shred the marrow and chop the prunes and place these together with the marrow seeds, sugar and rose-hips/shells into the initial fermentation vessel. Pour in the *boiling* water and stir well with a wooden spoon to dissolve the sugar. When cool add the juice of the lemons and yeast nutrient. Introduce the activated wine yeast and ferment on the "pulp" for 7 days, stirring the must daily with a wooden spoon and keep it closely covered. Then strain, for secondary fermentation, into a fermentation vessel and fit air-lock. Leave to ferment in the normal way, racking as necessary.

May (Hawthorn Blossom)

Ingredients:

> 2.25 litres (2 qt.) hawthorn flowers
> 1.5 kg (3½ lb.) white sugar
> 1 teaspoon tannin
>
> 4.5 litres (1 gal.)
> 2 lemons
> Yeast and nutrient

Method:

Boil up the sugar, flowers and lemon rind (no white pith) in water for 30 minutes, adding more water if necessary to retain the volume. Pour into a bucket and when cool add the yeast, the lemon juice, and the yeast nutrient. Leave for eight days, stirring daily, then strain through muslin into fermenting bottle and fit trap. Leave until it clears, then siphon off and bottle.

Meads

Ingredients:

1.8 kg (4 lb.) English honey   Yeast
4.5 litres (1 gal.) water   Yeast nutrient
1 lemon, 1 orange

Method:

Bring the honey in the water to the boil, and leave to cool in a bucket. Add the juice of the citrus fruit, the yeast nutrient, and the yeast, pour into a fermenting bottle and fit air-lock. Mead sometimes takes rather long to ferment but when it is clear and fermentation has ceased, siphon off into clean bottles and leave to mature.

MELOMEL (a fruit-flavoured mead)

Ingredients:

1.5 kg (3½ lb.) honey   Juice of 2 lemons
225 g (½ lb.) dried rose-hips   Yeast and nutrient
Water to 4.5 litres (1 gal.)

Method:

Soak the dried rose-hips in a little of the water for 24 hours. Then return them (and their water) to the rest of the ingredients, bring to the boil, and simmer for 10 minutes. Add the honey and stir until dissolved. Strain into a fermenting jar when cool, and add the juice of the two lemons and the yeast nutrient. When the temperature has dropped to 21°C (70°F) add the yeast, preferably a Maury yeast. Ferment and rack as usual. Mead fermentations, it should be noted, are often rather lengthy.

MELOMEL APERITIF

Ingredients:

2.25 litres (4 pt.) orange juice	**Nutrients**
Peel from 12 oranges	**Madeira yeast starter**
570 ml (1 pt.) white grape concentrate	**Water to 4.5 litres (1 gal.)**
675 g (1½ lb.) clover honey	

Method:

Express the juice from sufficient oranges to give 2.5 litres (4 pt.) orange juice. Add the grape concentrate, dissolve the honey in this blend and make the volume up to 4.5 litres (1 gal.) with water. Add the nutrients and 100 p.p.m. sulphite (2 Campden tablets). After 24 hours, introduce the yeast and the peel from 12 oranges (no pith should be included). Ferment to dryness and thereafter proceed as directed in the basic procedure, removing the orange peel at the first racking. Fortification may be practised if desired.

TABLE MELOMEL

Ingredients:

3.75 litres (6 pt.) pear juice	**Nutrients**
570 ml (1 pt.) white grape concentrate	**Champagne yeast starter**
450 g (1 lb.) acacia blossom honey	**Water to 4.5 litres (1 gal.)**
280 ml (½ pt.) yellow rose petals	

Method:

Express the juice from sufficient pears, 6 kg (12–14 lb.) to give 3.75 litres (6 pt.) juice. Dissolve the honey and nutrients in this juice and add 100 p.p.m. sulphite (2 Campden tablets). After 24 hours add the yeast starter. Allow to ferment for seven days, then add the rose petals. After a further three days, strain off the rose

"Don't you think you're drinking too much mead, Henry?"

petals and make the volume up to 4.5 litres (1 gal.) with water. Ferment to dryness and thereafter proceed as instructed in the basic procedure.

Note: An excellent sparkling wine can be made from this recipe by reducing the amount of honey to 335 g (¾ lb.) and using honey instead of sugar to prime the bottles prior to the bottle fermentation. Careful control is necessary to be successful here, but outstanding sparkling wines can be obtained in this manner, especially if perry pears are available. For full details of sparkling wine production – see the companion books in this series – *Making Wines Like Those You Buy* and *Those You Buy* and *How to make Wines With A Sparkle.*

PIPPIN CYSER

Ingredients:

4.5 litres (1 gal.) Cox's Orange Pippin juice	**Nutrients**
	Sauternes yeast starter
900 g (2 lb.) acacia blossom honey	

Method:

Express the juice from sufficient Cox's Orange Pippins to give 4.5 litres (1 gal.) of juice (about 7.2 kg (16 lb.) apples required). Dissolve the honey in this juice, add 100 p.p.m. sulphite (2 Campden tablets) and leave to settle for 24 hours. Rack off the juice from the sediment which has been deposited, then add the nutrients and yeast starter. Ferment until the gravity drops to 12 and rack. Rack again as soon as fermentation restarts and add 50 p.p.m. sulphite (1 Campden tablet). Thereafter bottle and mature as usual.

Note: This wine will mature well and 45 litre (10 gal.) quantities will benefit from spending 6–12 months in cask prior to bottling. Most winemakers will be unable to make this quantity, of course, but those who can will never regret doing so!

"I'm making mead"

ROSE CYSER

Ingredients:

2.25 kg (4 pt.) apple juice
570 ml (1 pt.) white grape concentrate
280 ml (½ pt.) yellow rose petals

450 g (1 lb.) clover honey
Nutrients
Steinberg yeast starter

Method:

Express the juice from sufficient apples 4 kg (8–10 lb.) to give 2.25 kg (½ gal.) juice. Add 115 ml (2 pt.) water and dissolve the honey and nutrients in the diluted apple juice. Add 100 p.p.m. sulphite (2 Campden tablets) and leave to settle for 24 hours. Blend in the grape concentrate and introduce the yeast. After seven days add the rose petals and strain off three days later. Make the volume up to 4.5 litres (1 gal.) with water, ferment to dryness and thereafter continue as directed in the basic procedure.

Note: An interesting variation which gives a rosé wine can be tried by substituting part of the grape concentrate and/or yellow rose petals by red grape concentrate and red rose petals. Canned apple juice can also be used in place of fresh apple juice if desired.

Morello

Ingredients:

3.6 kg (8 lb.) cracked and windfall
  Morello cherries
Water to 4.5 litres (1 gal.)

1.5 kg (3½ lb.) sugar
Yeast and nutrient

Method:

Stalk and wash the fruit, place in a crock, and add 570 ml (1 pt.) of cold water to each 450 g (1 lb.) of fruit, and then one crushed Campden tablet per 4.5 litres (1 gal.). Lastly add a level teaspoonful of dried yeast. Leave for 10 days, keeping closely covered, but stir well each day and mash the fruit with the hands. Strain mixture through nylon sieve into fermentation jar, add the sugar, and top up with water. Agitate well to dissolve sugar. When vigorous fermentation dies down, fit air-lock. Ferment out, rack, and bottle in usual way.

Mulberry

Ingredients:

4 kg (9 lb.) mulberries (this wine needs a heavy fruit content)
450 g (1 lb.) raisins
1.3 kg (3 lb.) sugar
2 lemons
Pectic enzyme
Water to finally make up 4.5 litres (1 gal.) of "must"
Yeast nutrient and activated wine yeast

Method:

Place the mulberries, chopped raisins and sugar into the initial fermentation vessel, and crush the mulberries by stirring with a wooden spoon. Then pour in the *boiling* water and stir to dissolve the sugar. When cool (20°C, 70°F) add the lemon juice, pektolase and yeast nutrient. Introduce the activated wine yeast (Burgundy or Port wine yeasts are suggested) and ferment on the "pulp" for 7 days, stirring each day with a wooden spoon and ensuring that the "must" is closely covered. Then strain into the secondary fermentation vessel and leave to ferment under the protection of a fermentation lock, racking as necessary.

Mulls

"How you totter, good feet! Have a care of my bones! If you fail me, I pass all the night on these stones"
— William Terrington.

MULLED ALE (to make 9 wine glasses)

Ingredients:

1 litre (2 pt.) ale (brown ale is best)
1 tablespoon caster sugar

1 pinch each of ground cloves, nutmeg, ginger
1 wineglass rum or brandy

Method:

Put ale, sugar and spices in saucepan and bring nearly to boiling point. Add brandy or rum and serve at once while still very hot.

MULLED CIDER

Ingredients:

4.5 litres (1 gal.) cider
1½ cups brown sugar
½ teaspoonful ginger
1½ teaspoonful of cloves

1½ teaspoonsful of allspice
1½ sticks of cinnamon
½ teaspoonful nutmeg
½ teaspoonful salt

Method:

Place the sugar, spices, cider and salt into the saucepan, heat and simmer for 20 minutes, strain through muslin or fine nylon strainer and rinse out saucepan. Then return the strained liquor to the saucepan and reheat until piping hot (avoid boiling). Serves 15 beakers or mugs according to size. Hot mulled cider is an excellent "goodnight friends" drink on a chilly night.

MULLED CIDER

Ingredients:

1 litre (1 qt.) cider
3 eggs

Sugar to taste

Method:

Add the sugar to the cider to adjust acidity to taste and bring to almost boiling point. Pour the heated liquor over the whisked eggs and stir well. Return the mixture to the saucepan and reheat and serve in glasses piping hot.

MULLED ELDERBERRY

Ingredients:

1 bottle medium sweet
    elderberry wine
55 g (2 oz.) loaf sugar
3 or 4 cloves

2.5 cm (1 in.) stick of cinnamon
½ teaspoon allspice
Orange and lemon rind
Angostura bitters

Method:

Pour the wine into a sound enamel saucepan, add sugar, cloves, spices and a few curls of orange and lemon rind. Heat without

94

boiling and strain into a warm jug. Add half teaspoon Angostura bitters and a little hot water to taste. Serve with a pinch of nutmeg in earthenware mugs.

MULLED STOUT (and ale too!)

Method:

Pour the stout or ale into a pewter tankard and immerse a red hot poker. Take precautions to avoid overflowing!

VINTNERS' MULL

Ingredients:

1 bottle sweet wine	**Ground ginger**
1 wine glass apricot brandy	**Caster sugar**
1 large sweet orange	**280 ml (½ pt.) boiling water**

Method:

Stud the orange with the cloves and bake for one hour. Heat the wine, brandy and ginger to almost boiling point – remember *boiling* drives off the alcohol and robs the brew of its potency – with the baked orange floating on top and add the sugar to suit one's own taste – a further 280 ml (½ pt.) of *boiling* water may be added just before serving – if you are feeling economical.

WASSAIL BOWL

"In the Wassail Bowl we'll drink unto thee Wassail! Wassail! Wassail!"

Ingredients:

1 litre (1 qt.) beer or ale	**A few slices of lemond rind**
¼ teaspoonful ginger	**(no pith)**
¼ teaspoonful nutmeg	**280 ml (½ pt.) sherry**
¼ teaspoonful ground	**Sugar to taste**
cinnamon	**6 crab apples or 3 rosy red apples**

Method:

Heat the sherry and ale together with the spices and lemon rind and simmer for five minutes. Prior to this bake the apples until they are just soft and baste well whilst cooking with ale and sugar. Then add these to the spiced liquor, adding extra sugar to taste. Serve really piping hot in tankards.

The foregoing are just a few examples of how you can vary the method of serving your home-made wines, ciders and beers, but remember if you are drinking alcohol in quantity you will need something to eat!

Meadowsweet
(Filipendula Ulmaria)

"The floures boiled in wine and drunke, do make the heart merrie"
– Gerrard.

Ingredients:

> 4.5 litres (1 gal.) meadowsweet flowers (heads only) (or 55 g (2 oz.) packet dried heads
> 450 g (1 lb.) raisins (dried figs, dates, prunes, or apricots, etc., may be substituted)
> 1.3 kg (3 lb.) sugar
> 280 ml (½ pt.) strong tea (or a pinch of grape tannin)
> 15 g (½ oz.) Citric acid (or 3 lemons, no pith, in lieu)
> Water to finally make up 4.5 litres (1 gal.) "must"
> Yeast nutrient and activated wine yeast

Method:

Place the flowers, chopped fruit, and sugar into the initial fermentation vessel. Pour in the *boiling* water and stir well with a wooden spoon to dissolve the sugar, etc. When cool add the citric acid, strong tea and yeast nutrient. Introduce the activated wine yeast and ferment on the "pulp" for 7 days, stirring the "must" daily with a woden spoon and keep it closely covered. Then strain for secondary fermentation, in a fermentation vessel and fit airlock. Leave to ferment in the normal way, racking as necessary.

96

Meadowsweet and Banana

Ingredients:

Meadowsweet herb *(Filipendula ulmaria)*
450 g (1 lb.) fresh herb or 55 g (2 oz.) dried herb
110 g (4 oz.) dried bananas (or 900 g (2 lb.) fresh bananas with skins)
450 g (1 lb.) raisins or sultanas
1.3 kg (3 lb.) sugar (or 1.8 kg (3½ lb.) honey)
10 g (¼ oz.) citric acid (or 2 lemons, no pith in lieu)
3 g ($^1/_{10}$ oz.) grape tannin (or 280 ml (½ pt.) strong tea)
Water to make up finally 4.5 litres (1 gal.) of "must"
Yeast nutrient and activated wine yeast

Method:

Place the herb, chopped fruits and sugar into the initial fermentation vessel. Pour in the *boiling* water and stir with a wooden spoon to dissolve the sugar, etc. When cool add the citric acid, grape tannin and yeast nutrient. Introduce the activated wine yeast and ferment on the "pulp" for 7 days, stirring the "must" with a wooden spoon, daily, ensuring that the "must" is closely covered. Then strain, for secondary fermentation, into fermentation vessel, and fit air-lock. Leave to ferment in the normal way, racking as necessary in due course.

Medlar and Rosehip

Ingredients:

1.3 kg (3 lb.) medlars (picked November and stored 3 weeks or so until almost overripe)
225 g (8 oz.) dried rose-hips or 113 g (4 oz.) shells
55 g (2 oz.) dried bananas (or 450 g (1 lb.) bananas including skins)
1.3 kg (3 lb.) sugar (or 1.8 kg (4 lb.) honey)
15 g (½ oz.) citric acid (or 3 lemons, no pith, in lieu)
280 ml (½ pt.) strong tea (or a pinch of grape tannin)
Pectic enzyme
Water to finally make up 4.5 litres (1 gal.) of "must"
Yeast nutrient and activated wine yeast

Method:

It is essential to store the medlars until almost overripe because the slightly acid taste is not brought out until they have been stored for three weeks or more.

Place the fruits, together with the sugar, into the initial fermentation vessel. Pour in the *boiling* water. Macerate and stir well with a wooden spoon to break up the fruit and to dissolve the sugar. When cool, add the citric acid, strong tea, pektolase and yeast nutrients. Introduce the activated wine yeast and ferment on the "pulp" for 7 days stirring the "must" daily with a wooden spoon and keep it closely covered. Then strain for secondary fermentation, into fermentation vessel, and fit air-lock. Leave to ferment in the normal way, racking as necessary.

Mint

Ingredients:

850 ml (1½ pt.) mint leaves (lightly bruised)
280 ml (½ pt.) strong tea
1.5 kg (3½ lb.) sugar
2 lemons or 10 g (¼ oz.) citric acid
Yeast nutrient
Yeast
Water to produce 4.5 litres (1 gal.)

Method:

Pour *boiling* water over the sugar and mint leaves. Stir well. Infuse or 24 hours, then add the lemon juice, yeast and nutrient. Forty-eight hours later strain into fermentation jar and make up to 4.5 litres (1 gal.) if necessary. Ferment, rack and bottle as usual.

Mint Surprise

Ingredients:

110–165 g (4–6 oz.) well-bruised mint leaves, including chopped
    stalks (45 g (1½ oz.) dried mint may be used in lieu)
1.3 kg (3 lb.) rhubarb
Water to 4.5 litres (1 gal.)
450 g (1 lb.) barley or wheat (crushed)
280 ml (½ pt.) strong tea
1.8 kg (4 lb.) sugar
Yeast nutrient and selected wine yeast

Method:

Soak the grain in 570 ml (1 pt.) of water overnight, then run
through a mincer. Add the crushed rhubarb. Boil the mint in
4.5 litres (1 gal.) of water for 15 minutes, then pour over the grain
and rhubarb, add sugar, stir well. When cool add the strong tea.
Then add the yeast nutrient and activated wine yeast. Ferment on
solids 7–10 days, then strain into fermentation vessel and allow to
finish in normal way.

Minteano

Recipe by the late Mr. F. G. Spark, of Andover, who specialised
in spiced and unusual wines:

"Save tea left over from the teapot until you have nearly 850 ml
(1½ pt.), then add 165 g (6 oz.) sugar and 55 g (2 oz.) chopped
raisins or sultanas and a saltspoon of a good quality dried yeast,
and cork lightly or plug with cotton wool. This will start to ferment and thus save mould growing on the surface of the "must"
while you are collecting another litre or more in other bottles until
you have 4.5 litres (1 gal.), using the same amount of sugar and
raisins for each litre. When you have your gallon add a handful
of chopped mint and the juice of two lemons or one level
teaspoonful of citric acid, fit air-lock and ferment for one month,
then strain, and proceed in the usual manner until fermentation
ceases. Keep for one year and you will have a very fine and unusual
wine."

Mixed Soft Fruit

Ingredients:

**2.7 kg (5 lb.) any soft fruit – mixed or otherwise 560 g (1¼ lb.)
  dried bilberries may be used instead).
2 litres (4 pt.) cider
30 g (1 oz.) root ginger
1 teaspoonful each dried rosemary and lavender leaves (optional)
35 g (1¼ oz.) cream of tartar
1.3 kg (3 lb.) sugar (or 1.8 kg (4 lb.) honey)
3 g ($^1/_{10}$ oz.) grape tannin (or 280 ml (½ pt.) strong tea)
Yeast nutrient and activated wine yeast
Water: sufficient to produce 4.5 litres (1 gal.) of "must"**

Method:

Prepare the fruits, ensuring that there are no leaves or stalks
used. Macerate with a wooden spoon, then add the root ginger,
herbs, if used, and sugar and place these in the initial fermentation
vessel. Pour in 1 litre (2 pt.) of *boiling* water and stir well to dissolve
the sugar. When cool add the cream of tartar, tannin, yeast
nutrient, cider and activated wine yeast. Cover well and ferment
five days, then strain through a nylon sieve into glass fermentation
bottles. Fit air-lock and leave to ferment in normal way, racking as
necessary in due course. The use of mixed fruits gives a better
"balance" than using a single fruit.

Variations:

225 g (½ lb.) of malt extract may be used as an additive to give
"body".

Nectarine

Ingredients:

1.5 g (3½ lb.) nectarines (or peaches in lieu)
55 g (2 oz.) dried bananas
1.3 kg (3 lb.) sugar
15 g (½ oz.) citric acid (or 3 lemons, no pith, in lieu)
280 ml (½ pt.) strong tea (or a pinch of grape tannin)
Pectic enzyme
Water to finally make up 4.5 litres (1 gal.) of "must"
Yeast nutrient and activated wine yeast

Method:

Clean and stone the nectarines and place these together with the dried bananas and sugar into the initial fermentation vessel. Pour in the *boiling* water, macerate and stir well with a wooden spoon to break up the fruit and to dissolve the sugar. When cool add the citric acid, strong tea, pectinol and yeast nutrient. Introduce the activated wine yeast and ferment on the "pulp" for 7 days, stirring the "must" daily with a wooden spoon and keep it closely covered. Then strain, for secondary fermentation, into fermentation vessel and fit air-lock. Leave to ferment in the normal way, racking as necessary.

Oak leaf

Ingredients:

60 young oak leaves
1.3 kg (3 lb.) sugar
3 lemons
3 oranges or 15 g (½ oz.) citric acid

Yeast nutrient
Selected wine yeast
Water to 4.5 litres (1 gal.)

Method:

Cleanse the leaves by swirling them in cold water and drain off. Pour the 4.5 litres (1 gal.) of *boiling* water over the leaves and allow them to infuse for 24 hours. Strain, then simmer the liquid to obtain sufficient heat to enable liquid to dissolve the sugar. Pour the hot extract over the sugar, add the lemon and orange juices or citric acid, and stir well. The grated peel of the oranges (no pith) should be simmered in a little of the liquid for 15 minutes and the resulting liquid is then returned to the bulk. When cool make up to 4.5 litres (1 gal.) again with water, if necessary, add the yeast nutrient, introduce an activated general purpose wine yeast and allow fermentation to proceed (using air-locks) in the normal way. Fully matured leaves or leaves in early autumn that are changing colour may be used to give variations, as may walnut leaves.

Onion

Ingredients:

225 g (½ lb.) onions	**1 teaspoon tannin**
225 g (½ lb.) potatoes	**2 lemons or citric acid**
450 g (1 lb.) chopped raisins	**Yeast nutrient**
1.3 kg (3 lb.) sugar	**Yeast (selected wine)**
Water to 4.5 litres (1 gal.)	

Method:

Slice and dice the onions and potatoes and place these together with the chopped raisins in warm (not hot) water in which the sugar has been dissolved. Add lemon juice (no pith) or citric acid and yeast nutrient, then introduce activated yeast. Ferment for 10 days, then strain and complete fermentation in glass jars under fermentation lock.

Orange Peel (dried)

Ingredients:

570 ml (1 pt.) of pieces of dried peel	**1.1 kg (2½ lb.) sugar**
5 g (¼ oz.) root ginger	**Water to 4.5 litres (1 gal.)**
450 g (½ lb.) raisins or sultanas	**Yeast and nutrient**

Method:

Pour the *boiling* water over the peel and leave for three days. Remove the peel and add ginger, raisins and sugar, and ferment with wine yeast. When fermentation quietens, after about a week, strain into fermenting jar and fit trap. The 1.1 kg (2½ lb.) sugar gives a dry wine and this quantity can be increased if required.

Seville Orange

Ingredients:

12 thin skinned Seville oranges
2 lemons
1.5 kg (3½ lb.) sugar
Pectic enzyme

Water to 4.5 litres (1 gal.)
Yeast and nutrient

Method:

Peel six of the oranges and throw away the peel. Cut up oranges and lemons into slices and put into earthenware pan. Boil the water and pour on boiling. Place in moderately warm corner and when tepid add yeast, a good wine yeast or a level teaspoonful of granulated yeast; stir each day for a fortnight. Strain all through a sieve, then add sugar and stir until dissolved. Put in 4.5 litre (1 gal.) jar, filling up to top. Put surplus in dark bottles (bottles must be coloured or wine will lose its colour). Use this for filling up large jar. Ferment to completion under air-lock, rack when it clears, and bottle two months later.

Orange and Banana

Ingredients:

10 oranges
450 g (1 lb.) bananas (or 55 g (2 oz.) dried variety)
225 g (½ lb.) raisins (or sultanas)
140 ml (¼ pt.) strong tea
1.3 kg (3 lb.) sugar
Yeast nutrient and activated wine yeast
Water: sufficient to finally produce 4.5 litres (1 gal.) of "must"

Method:

Peel the oranges very thinly, avoiding the white pith which imparts very undesirable bitterness. Cut the oranges in half and squeeze out the juice. Place the juice and remainder of the fruit, minus the pith, together with the chopped bananas and raisins into the initial fermentation vessel. Add the sugar and pour in three-quarters of the water almost boiling hot, and stir with a wooden spoon to dissolve the sugar. The remaining quart of water should be placed in a saucepan together with the orange peel and this be allowed to simmer for 30 minutes. When cool (20°C, 70°F) add the strong tea and yeast nutrient. Introduce the activated wine yeast cover securely and leave to ferment for 7 days on the pulp, stirring occasionally, then strain into secondary fermentation vessel. Fit air-lock and leave to ferment in the normal way racking as necessary.

Orange and Raisin

Ingredients:

3 Jaffa oranges	450 g (1 lb.) raisins
3 Seville oranges	1.3 kg (3 lb.) sugar
6 sweet oranges	Water to 4.5 litres (1 gal.)
2 lemons	Yeast nutrient and activated
Pectic enzyme	wine yeast

Method:

Peel the oranges and lemons very thinly and discard the pith. Put the skins into oven, and bake them until they are browned, then pour over them a litre (1 qt.) of *boiling* water and infuse as for making tea. Place the sugar into the initial fermentation vessel, add boiling water to dissolve sugar. When cool add the chopped raisins, pulped oranges and lemons, and the infusion from the skins. Add the yeast nutrient and activated wine yeast. Ferment on the "pulp" for 7 days then strain into fermentation bottles. Fit air-lock and leave to ferment in the normal way, racking as necessary.

Parsley

Ingredients:

450 g (1 lb.) fresh parsley
1.3 kg (3 lb.) sugar
Water to 4.5 litres (1 gal.)

Lump of ginger
2 lemons
Yeast and nutrient
1 teaspoon tannin

Method:

Well wash and boil parsley until tender, strain into an earthenware crock. Add sugar, ginger and sliced lemons. Stir well until the sugar is dissolved. When cooled to blood heat add yeast and leave closely covered for a fortnight, stirring daily. Then strain into fermenting jar and fit trap. Siphon off when wine has cleared and keep for at least a further six months.

Parsley and Apricot

Ingredients:

450 g (1 lb.) fresh parsley, including stalks (or 1 packet of dried parsley)
450 g (1 lb.) dried apricots (or 1.3 kg (3 lb.) fresh apricots)
55 g (2 oz.) dried bananas (or dried rose-hips/shells)
1.3 kg (3 lb.) sugar
280 ml (½ pt.) strong tea (or a pinch of grape tannin)
2 lemons
Pectic enzyme
Water to finally make up 4.5 litres (1 gal.) of "must"
Yeast nutrient and activated wine yeast

Method:

Cut up the parsley and simmer for 20 minutes. Place the chopped fruits and sugar into the initial fermentation vessel, then pour in the parsley and parsley liquor. Stir well with a wooden spoon to dissolve the sugar. When cool add the lemon juice, strong tea, pectolase and yeast nutrient. Introduce the activated wine yeast, and ferment on the "pulp" for 7 days, stirring the "must" daily with a wooden spoon and keep it closely covered. Then strain, for secondary fermentation, into a fermentation vessel and fit air-lock. Leave to ferment in the normal way, racking as necessary.

Parsley and Balm

Ingredients:

> **450 g (1 lb.) fresh parsley, including stalks (or ½ packet dried parsley)**
> **225 g (½ lb.) fresh balm leaves (or ½ packet dried balm leaves)**
> **450 g (1 lb.) raisins (or mixed dried fruit, curants, or sultanas, etc.)**
> **55 g (2 oz.) dried bananas (optional) or dried rose-hips/shells**
> **1.3 kg (3 lb.) sugar**
> **280 ml (½ pt.) strong tea (or a pinch of grape tannin)**
> **1 level teaspoon citric acid (or 2 lemons, no pith, in lieu)**
> **Water to finally make up 4.5 litres (1 gal.) of "must"**
> **Yeast Nutrient and activated wine yeast**

Method:

Chop or bruise the herbs and place these with the chopped fruits and sugar into the initial fermentation vessel. Pour in the *boiling* water and stir well with a wooden spoon to dissolve the sugar. When cool add all the other ingredients. Ferment on the "pulp" for 7 days, then strain into fermentation jar, fit air-lock and ferment out, rack and bottle as usual.

Parsley and Carrot

Ingredients:

450 g (1 lb.) parsley (fresh) or 1 packet dried parsley
1.3 kg (3 lb.) carrots
1.1 kg (2½ lb.) sugar
15 g (½ oz.) citric acid (or 3 lemons, no pith, in lieu)
280 ml (½ pt.) strong tea (or 3 g ($^1/_{10}$ oz.) grape tannin)
Yeast nutrient and activated wine yeast
Water: sufficient to finally produce 4.5 litres (1 gal.) of "must"

Method:

Scrape the young carrots and cut in two length-ways. Cook these 80% in 2 litres (4 pt.) of water. Have ready *boiling* water in which to place the carrots after straining carrot essence on to sugar in the initial fermentation vessel. The carrots when transferred to the second vessel to which salt is added may then be finally cooked and eaten. In a separate vessel bring 1 litre (2 pt.) of water to the boil and add the bruised and lightly chopped parsley. When this has boiled half a minute leave to infuse for one hour then strain into the sugared carrot essence. When cool add the acid, strong tea, yeast nutrient and activated wine yeast. Cover closely and ferment for three days, then transfer through nylon sieve to fermentation vessel and top up with water if necessary. Fit air-lock and ferment in normal way, racking as necessary in due course. A pleasant light, dry table wine.

Parsley and Rice

Ingredients:

450 g (1 lb.) parsley (or small packet dried variety)
900 g (2 lb.) paddy rice with husks (or barley)
450 g (1 lb.) raisins (sultanas, figs, apricots, etc., may be used instead)
15 g (½ oz.) citric acid (or 3 lemons, no pith, in lieu)
3 g ($^1/_{10}$ oz.) grape tannin (or 280 ml (½ pt.) strong tea)
1.3 kg (3 lb.) sugar (or 1.8 kg (4 lb.) honey)
Yeast nutrient and activated wine yeast
Water: sufficient to finally produce 4.5 litres (1 gal.) of "must"

Method:

Cut up the parsley into small pieces and place in the initial fermentation vessel together with the paddy rice, dried fruits and sugar. Pour in the *boiling* water and stir well to dissolve the sugar. When cool add the acid, tannin, yeast nutrient and introduce the activated wine yeast. Cover securely and leave to ferment for 10 days, then strain into fermentation bottles and fit air lock. Leave to ferment in normal way, racking as necessary.

Variations:

1. 1 litre (1 qt.) cider instead of dried fruit (to be added to "must" when cool).
2. Use 1 bottle of Roses Lime juice instead of dried fruit – again add only to the "must" when cool.

Parsnip

Ingredients:

450 g (1 lb.) parsnips	**450 g (1 lb.) raisins or sultanas**
Water to 4.5 litres (1 gal.)	**2 oranges**
1.8 kg (4 lb.) sugar	**2 lemons**
Yeast and nutrient	**1 teaspoon tannin**

Method:

Scrub and slice the parsnips and put into a large pan with 3 litres (6 pt.) of the water. Bring to the boil and simmer for five minutes. Remove the scum as it rises. Strain through nylon sieve into a bowl and discard the "pulp". Add 900 g (2 lb.) of the sugar and stir until it is dissolved. Chop the raisins and cut the oranges and lemons into small pieces. Put them in parsnip mixture. When liquid is cool, add the yeast nutrient. Cover the bowl with polythene and leave ten days for the first fermentation. Strain through muslin into a bucket.

Put 900 g (2 lb.) sugar into pan with 2 litres (4 pt.) of water, bring to the boil and simmer for two minutes. Allow to cool, then stir into the liquor. Pour liquid through a funnel into a glass jar, fit a cork and airlock and leave until second fermentation has ceased, rack and bottle wine.

Parsnip and Apricot

Ingredients:

1.8–2.7 kg (4–6 lb.) parsnips
450 g (1 lb.) dried apricots
1 litre (2 pt.) commercial or home-made cider (or ¼ bottle Vierka concentrated "must")
1.5 kg (3½ lb.) sugar
15 g (½ oz.) citric acid (or 3 lemons, no pith, in lieu)
280 ml (½ pt.) cold strong tea (or a pinch of grape tannin)
Water to make up 4.5 litres (1 gal.) "must"
Yeast nutrient and activated wine yeast

Method:

Simmer gently in half the water the scrubbed and thinly sliced parsnips, until slightly tender. Place the chopped apricots and sugar into the initial fermentation vessel: strain into this the hot parsnip liquor. Stir to dissolve the sugar. When cool add the cold tea or grape tannin and citric acid or lemon juice; add the cider and the remainder of the water to make up 4.5 litres (1 gal.) of "must". Add the yeast nutrient and then introduce the activated wine yeast. Ferment on the "pulp" for 7 days then strain into fermentation bottles. Fit air lock and leave to ferment in normal way, racking as necessary.

Parsnip and Beetroot

Ingredients:

   1.8 kg (4 lb.) parsnips
   900 g (2 lb.) beetroot
   225 g (½ lb) or 450 g (1 lb.) malt extract
   280 ml (½ pt.) cold strong tea
   1.8 kg (4 lb.) sugar
   15 g (½ oz.) citric acid (or 3 lemons, no pith, in lieu)
   Water to 4.5 litres (1 gal.)
   Yeast nutrient and activated wine yeast

Method:

Wash the roots well – do not peel – slice thinly and simmer gently until slightly tender. Place the sugar and malt extract into a polythene bucket or crock vessel, then strain into this the hot liquor from the roots and stir until the sugar and malt is dissolved. When cool add the cold strong tea and citric acid. Then add the yeast nutrient and introduce the activated wine yeast. Cover well and three days later strain into fermentation vessels. Fit air-lock and leave to ferment in normal way, racking as necessary.

Parsnip and Birch Sap

Ingredients:

   1.3 kg (3 lb.) parsnips
   2.25 litres (½ gal.) of birch sap (see Birch Sap, p. 23)
   450 g (1 lb.) raisins (or other dried fruit)
   55 g (2 oz.) dried rose-hips/shells (or 55 g (2 oz.) dried bananas)
   1.3 kg (3 lb.) sugar or 1.8 kg (4 lb.) invert sugar
   140 ml (¼ pt.) strong tea (or ½ teaspoonful grape tannin)
   15 g (½ oz.) citric acid (or 3 lemons, no pith, in lieu)
   Water to finally make up 4.5 litres (1 gal.) of "must"
   Yeast and nutrient

Method:

Slice and simmer the old parsnips in 2 litres (4 pt.) of water in the normal way. Place the chopped raisins, rose-hips and half the sugar into the initial fermentation vessel and strain into this the hot parsnip liquor. Stir to dissolve the sugar. When cool (20°C, 70°F) add the chopped fruits, strong tea, citric acid, yeast nutrient, and introduce the activated wine yeast. Leave closely covered to ferment. In early March obtain 2.25 litres (½ gal.) of birch sap and heat this sufficiently to dissolve into it the balance of the sugar. When cool add this to the fermenting "must". After 7 days from commencement of fermentation, strain into secondary fermentation vessel. Fit air-lock and leave to ferment in the normal way, racking as necessary.

Variations:

1. Sycamore and walnut sap can be used in lieu.
2. Place 24 bruised young birch leaves in the fermenting "must" if the lemon-like fragrance attached to birch wood is desired.
3. If insufficient birch sap is available make up the difference with cider.

The making of birch sap wine, together with illustrations of the tapping of a birch tree is described in detail on page 29.

Parsnip and Date

Ingredients:

1.8–2.7 kg (4–6 lb.) parsnips
900 g (2 lb.) dates
55 g (2 oz.) dried bananas
1.3 kg (3 lb.) sugar
15 g (½ oz.) citric acid (or 3 lemons, no pith, in lieu)
280 ml (½ pt.) cold strong tea (or a pinch of grape tannin)
Water to make up 4.5 litres (1 gal.) of "must"
Yeast nutrient and activated wine yeast

Method:

Scrub and slice thinly the parsnips and simmer gently in half the water until slightly tender. Place the chopped dates, dried bananas and sugar into a polythene or crock vessel for initial fermentation, then strain into this the hot parsnip liquor. Stir to dissolve the sugar. When cool add the cold tea or grape tannin and citric acid or lemon juice. Add the remainder of the water to make up the necessary amount of "must", then add the yeast nutrient and introduce the activated wine yeast. Ferment on the "pulp" for 7 days then strain into fementation bottles. Fit air-lock and leave to ferment in normal way, racking as necessary.

Parsnip and Elderflower

Ingredients:

1.8 kg (4 lb.) parsnips
70 ml ($^1/_8$ pt.) each dried elderflowers and rose petals
3 grapefruit
450 g (1 lb.) raisins
1.3 kg (3 lb.) sugar
280 ml (½ pt.) strong tea (or a ½ teaspoon grape tannin)
15 g (½ oz.) citric acid (or 3 lemons, no pith)
Water to finally produce 4.5 litres (1 gal.) of "must"
Yeast nutrient and activated wine yeast

Method:

Simmer gently in half the water the scrubbed and thinly sliced parsnips until slightly tender, avoid over-cooking and do not press out. Peel the grapefruit very thinly and discard the pith. Put the skins into the oven, and bake them until they are browned, then pour over them a litre (1 qt.) of *boiling* water and infuse as in making tea. Place the sugar into the initial fermentation vessel and strain into this the hot parsnip liquor and stir to dissolve the sugar.

When cool (20°C, 70°F) add the chopped raisins, pulped grapefruit, dried elderflowers and infusion from the grapefruit skins. Add the tea, citric acid, yeast nutrient and introduce the activated wine yeast. Ferment closely covered, for 7 days, then strain into the secondary fermentation vessel. Fit air-lock and leave to ferment in the normal way, racking as necessary. Tinned grapefruit may be used in lieu of fresh fruit.

Parsnip and Fig

Ingredients:

1.8–2.7 kg (4–6 lb.) parsnips
900 g (2 lb.) dried figs
55 g (2 oz.) dried rose-hips/ shells
1.3 kg (3 lb.) sugar
Yeast nutrient and activated wine yeast

15 g (½ oz.) citric acid (or 3 lemons, no pith, in lieu)
280 ml (½ pt.) cold strong tea (or a pinch of grape tannin)
Water to make up 4.5 litres (1 gal.) "must"

Method:

Scrub the parsnips (which are best lifted after the first frost) but do not peel. Cut it into thin slices and simmer gently in half the water until slightly tender. Place the cut up dried figs, rose-hips (shells) and sugar into a polythene bucket or crock vessel, then strain into this the hot parsnip liquor. Stir to dissolve the sugar. When cool add the cold tea or grape tannin and citric acid or lemon juice. Add the remainder of the water to make up the necessary amount of "must", then add the yeast nutrient and introduce the activated wine yeast. Ferment on the "pulp" for 7 days, then strain into fermentation bottles. Fit air-lock and leave to ferment in normal way, racking as necessary.

Parsnip and Orange

Ingredients:

1.3–1.8 kg (3–4 lb.) parsnips
6–8 oranges (see note below)
675 g (1½ lb.) raisins (or 280 ml (½ pt.) grape concentrate)
1.3 kg (3 lb.) sugar (dry wine) or 1.8 kg (4 lb.) sugar (sweet wine)
140 ml (¼ pt.) strong tea (or ½ teaspoonful grape tannin)
15 g (½ oz.) citric acid (or 3 lemons, no pith, in lieu)
Water to finally produce 4.5 litres (1 gal.) of "must"
Yeast nutrient and activated wine yeast

Method:

Scrub the parsnips (which are best lifted after the first frost) but do not peel. Cut into thin slices and simmer gently in half the water until slightly tender – avoid over boiling, otherwise difficulty may be experienced in clearing the wine. Peel the oranges very thinly and discard the pith. Put the skins into the oven, and bake them until they are browned then pour over them a quart of *boiling* water and infuse as in making tea. Place the sugar into the initial fermentation vessel and strain into this the hot parsnip liquor and stir to dissolve the sugar. When cool (20°C, 70°F) add the chopped raisins, pulped oranges and the infusion from the skins. Add the strong tea, citric acid, yeast nutrient and introduce the activated yeast. Ferment, closely covered, on the "pulp" for 10 days, then strain into the secondary fermentation vessel. Fit air-lock and leave to ferment in the normal way, racking later as necessary.

It is recognised generally that a mixture of varieties of Jaffa, Seville or sweet oranges and tangerines produces the most interesting results, but the use of one variety only is not detrimental to good results.

Parsnip and Rice

Ingredients:

    1.8–2.7 kg (4–6 lb.) parsnips
    1.3 kg (3 lb.) paddy rice, with husks (crushed maize, barley or
      wheat may be substituted)
    450 g (1 lb.) raisins or 280 ml (½ pt.) grape concentrate
    1.3 kg (3 lb.) sugar
    15 g (½ oz.) citric acid (or 3 lemons, no pith, in lieu)
    15 g (½ oz.) cold strong tea (or a pinch of grape tannin)
    Water to make up 4.5 litres (1 gal.) "must"
    Yeast nutrient and activated wine yeast

Method:

Scrub and thinly slice parsnips and simmer until slightly tender.
Pour the parsnip liquor over the paddy rice, chopped raisins and
sugar. Stir until sugar is dissolved and then when cool add the citric
acid and cold tea. Introduce the activated wine yeast and yeast
nutrient. Ferment on the "pulp" for 7 days, then strain into
fermentation bottles. Fit air lock and leave to ferment in normal
way, racking as necessary.

Parsnip and Peach

Ingredients:

    1.8 kg (4 lb.) parsnips
    1 tin peaches, (785 g (1 lb. 12 oz.) approx.) or 450 g (1 lb.) dried
      peaches
    900 g (2 lb.) bananas, including skins (or 55 g (1 lb.) dried
      bananas)
    1.3 kg (3 lb.) sugar
    A pinch of grape tannin
    15 g (½ oz.) citric acid (or 3 lemons, no pith, in lieu)
    Pectic enzyme
    Water to produce finally 4.5 litres (1 gal.) "must"
    Yeast nutrient and activated wine yeast

Method:

Do not peel the parsnips but scrub them well and slice thinly. Simmer gently in water until slightly tender. Place the tinned peaches and syrup (chop up dried peaches if used), chopped bananas and sugar into the initial fermentation vessel and strain into this the hot parsnip liquor. Stir well to dissolve the sugar, etc. When cool (20°C, 70°F) add the tannin, citric acid or lemon juice, Pectolase and yeast nutrient, and introduce the activated wine yeast. Cover closely, and leave to ferment for 7 days, stirring the "must" daily. Then strain into secondary fermentation vessel and fit air-lock. Leave to ferment in the normal way, racking when necessary.

Parsnip and Pineapple

Ingredients:

1.8 kg (4 lb.) parsnips
1 large or 2 small pineapples
450 g (1 lb.) raisins (or other dried fruits)
1.3 kg (3 lb.) sugar (or 1.8 kg (4 lb.) honey)
½ teaspoonful grape tannin
The juice of 2 lemons
Pectic enzyme
Water to make up 4.5 litres (1 gal.) of "must"
Yeast nutrient and activated wine yeast

Method:

Prepare the parsnip liquor in the normal way by *boiling* the sliced parsnips till tender, and straining. Place the chopped raisins, sugar and finely chopped pineapple into the initial fermentation vessel and pour in to this the hot parsnip liquor. Stir well to dissolve the sugar, etc. When cool (20°C, 70°F) add the tannin, lemon juice, Pectolase and yeast nutrient; introduce the activated wine yeast. Cover securely and leave to ferment for 7 days, stirring each day. Then strain into secondary fermentation vessel and ferment under protection of an air-lock in the normal way, racking as necessary.

Peach (dried)

Ingredients:

900 g (2 lb.) dried peaches
Water to 4.5 litres (1 gal.)
Yeast and nutrient

1.1 kg (2½ lb.) sugar
2 lemons
1 orange
1 teaspoon tannin

Method:

Wash peaches and soak overnight in 4.5 litres (1 gal.) of water. Bring to the oil and simmer until tender. Strain off hot liquid into jar containing the sugar (and use cooked peaches for serving cold with cream). Add the orange and lemon, thinly sliced and stir. When cool add the yeast and stir thoroughly. Leave for 7 days, stirring daily. Strain off into jar and fit air-lock.

Pear

Ingredients:

1.8 kg (4 lb.) pears
450 g (1 lb.) raisins
1.3 kg (3 lb.) sugar

1 teaspoon citric acid
Water to 4.5 litres (1 gal.)
Yeast and nutrient

Method:

Cut up the pears and chop the raisins. Pour over them the water, *boiling*, and then dissolve in the mixture 900 g (2 lb.) of the sugar; stir well. Allow to cool to 20°C (70°F) before adding the yeast and nutrient. Cover closely, and allow to stand in a warm place for 7 days, stirring daily, then strain, add the remaining sugar to the liquor, and pour into fermenting jar. Fit air-lock and ferment in temperature of 15–17°C (60–65°F) for about three months; then siphon the wine off the lees into a clean jar. Refit lock and leave for a further two months before bottling.

Pear and Apple

Ingredients:

1.8 kg (4 lb.) pears (really ripe ones)
1.8 kg (4 lb.) mixed apples (eating, cooking and crab if possible)
450 g (1 lb.) dried peaches (or apricots, figs, raisins, etc.)
55 g (2 oz.) dried rose-hips/shells
1.3 kg (3 lb.) sugar (or 1.8 kg (4 lb.) honey)
15 g (½ oz.) citric acid (or 3 lemons, no pith, in lieu)
Water to finally make up 4.5 litres (1 gal.) of "must"
Yeast nutrient and activated wine yeast
1 teaspoon grape tannin

Method:

Grate up the pears and apples, including cores and skins. Chop up the dried fruits, and these place together with the sugar into the initial fermentation vessel. Pour in the *boiling* water and stir with a wooden spoon to dissolve the sugar, etc. When cool add the citric acid, grape tannin and yeast nutrient. Introduce the activated wine yeast and ferment on the "pulp" for 7 days, stirring the "must" with a wooden spoon daily, ensuring that the "must" is closely covered. Then strain, for secondary fermentation into fermentation vessel, and fit air-lock. Leave to ferment in the normal way, racking as necessary.

Pineapple and Grape

Ingredients:

1 tin pineapple (775 g (1 lb. 12 oz.) approx.)
570 ml (1 pt.) concentrated grape juice (white)
½ teaspoonful citric acid or tartaric acid
70 ml (¹/₈ pt.) strong tea
1.1 kg (2½ lb.) sugar
Yeast nutrient and activated wine yeast
Water: sufficient to finally produce 4.5 litres (1 gal.) of "must"

"He drank a bottle of my hubby's pineapple wine"

Method:

Place the chopped pineapple and juice together with the grape concentrate in the initial fermentation vessel. Dissolve the sugar in hot water and add this to the fruit and grape concentrate. When cool (20°C, 70°F) add the strong tea, citric acid (or tartaric acid) and yeast nutrient. Introduce the activated wine yeast. Cover securely and leave to ferment for 7 days on the "pulp", stirring occasionally, then strain into the secondary fermentation vessel. Fit air-lock and leave to ferment in the normal way, racking later as necessary.

Variations:

1. 55 g (2 oz.) dried banana or 450 g (1 lb.) fresh bananas including skins may be added.
2. Substitute 900 g (2 lb.) chopped raisins/sultanas for grape concentrate.

Plum

Ingredients:

1.3 kg (3 lb.) plums	**1 teaspoon citric acid**
225 g (½ lb.) barley	**Water to 4.5 litres (1 gal.)**
1.5 kg (3½ lb.) sugar	**Yeast and nutrient**

Method:

Grind the barley in a mincer or coffee grinder and cut up the fruit, putting both into a bowl. Pour over them the *boiling* water, cover closely, and leave for four days, giving a vigorous stir twice daily. Then strain through nylon sieve on to the sugar, add the yeast nutrient, and stir till all is dissolved. Add the yeast, preferably a Burgundy wine yeast or a level teaspoon of granulated yeast. Keep closely covered in a warm place for a week, then pour into fermenting bottle, filling to bottom of neck, and fit air-lock. Siphon off for the first time when it clears but do not bottle until assured that fermentation has completely finished.

Pomegranate

Ingredients:

8 large pomegranates	1 teaspoon citric acid
1.3 kg (3 lb.) (plus) of sugar	Pectic enzyme
Water	G.P. wine yeast and nutrient

Method:

Take all the seeds out of the pomegranates, and remove the yellow skin. Press the pulp by hand in a muslin cloth and put the expressed juice into a bowl or polythene bucket. Boil up 900 g (2 lb.) of sugar in 2 litres (4 pt.) of water and pour on to the juice. When cool add Pectolase, nutrient, ½ teaspoon citric acid and G.P. wine yeast. Ferment in the warmth, covered, for seven days. Then boil up 450 g (1 lb.) of sugar in 1.7 litres (3 pt.) of water and put all into fermentation jar, fit air-lock, and ferment on. When the S.G. drops below 1.020, feed it with small amounts of sugar. Final S.G. should be about 1.018.

Prune

Ingredients:

900 g (2 lb.) prunes	1.3 kg (3 lb.) sugar
Water to 4.5 litres (1 gal.)	Yeast and nutrient
225 g (½ lb.) raisins	2 lemons

Method:

Pour the cold water over the prunes and chopped raisins, add a crushed Campden tablet, and let them stand for 10 days, stirring and mashing the fruit daily, then strain, being careful to extract all the liquid from the fruit before discarding it. Pour the liquor over the sugar, stir well to dissolve, add the juice of the lemon, and put the "must" into a fermenting jar. Add the yeast and yeast nutrient. Leave to ferment out (about two months) and rack into a clean jar when clear. Rack again after a further three months into clean bottles. This makes an excellent medium wine; for a dry wine reduce the sugar to 1.1 kg (2½ lb.).

Prune and Date

Ingredients:

  450 g (1 lb.) prunes
  450 g (1 lb.) dates
  450 g (1 lb.) sultanas (or raisins, currants, etc.)
  15 g (½ oz.) citric acid (or 3 lemons, no pith, in lieu)
  280 ml (½ pt.) strong tea (or a pinch of grape tannin)
  1.1 kg (2½ lb.) sugar (or 1.3 kg (3 lb.) honey)
  Water to finally make up 4.5 litres (1 gal.) of "must"
  Yeast and nutrient and activated wine yeast

Method:

Chop up the dried fruits and place these together with the sugar into the initial fermentation vessel. Pour in the *boiling* water and stir with a wooden spoon to dissolve the sugar, etc. When cool, add the strong tea, citric acid and yeast nutrient. Introduce the activated wine yeast and ferment on the "pulp" for 7 days, stirring the "must" with a wooden spoon daily, ensuring that the "must" is closely covered. Then strain, for secondary fermentation, into fermentation vessel, and fit air-lock. Leave to ferment in the normal way, racking as necessary.

Prune and Grape Concentrate

Ingredients:

  450 g (1 lb.) prunes
  570 ml (1 pt.) grape concentrate (white or red)
  110 g (4 oz.) dried rose-hips/shells (or 90 g (3 oz.) dried bananas)
  1.1 kg (2½ lb.) sugar
  15 g (½ oz.) citric acid (or 3 lemons, no pith, in lieu)
  140 ml (¼ pt.) strong tea (or a pinch of grape tannin)
  Yeast nutrient and activated wine yeast
  Water: sufficient to finally produce 4.5 litres (1 gal.) of "must"

Method:

Place the chopped fruits and rose-hips/shells and the sugar into the initial fermentation vessel and pour in the *boiling* water. Stir well with a wooden spoon to dissolve the sugar, then stir in the grape concentrate. When cool (20°C, 70°F) add the citric acid, strong tea, yeast nutrient, and introduce the activated wine yeast. Cover securely and leave to ferment for 7 days, then strain (by siphoning into a nylon strainer held in the funnel) into the secondary fermentation bottle and fit air-lock. Leave to ferment in the normal way, racking later as necessary.

Prune and Rhubarb

Ingredients:

900 g (2 lb.) prunes　　　　　　**1.3 kg (3 lb.) sugar**
1.3 kg (3 lb.) rhubarb　　　　　**Yeast and nutrient**
Cold water to 4.5 litres (1 gal.)

Method:

Cut the rhubarb into small pieces and put it into a bowl with the prunes, and cover with the water, cold. Add one Campden tablet. After 24 hours add the yeast and nutrient, and stir in 450 g (1 lb.) sugar. Ferment on the "pulp" for 10 days, mashing the fruit with the hands and giving it a good stir each day. On the seventh day stir in the remainder of the sugar, and on the 11th day strain the liquor into a fermentation jar and fit an air-lock. Press any juice out of the fruit, and include that, and also see to it that the fermentation jar is full, topping up with cold water if necessary. Ferment out, racking when the wine clears, and again 2–3 months later, this time into bottles.

Punches

ALE PUNCH

Ingredients:

1 litre (2 pt.) ale	30 g (1 oz.) sugar cubes
115 ml (1 gill) rum	3 cloves
115 ml (1 gill) gin	Nutmeg
115 ml (1 gill) whisky	Cinnamon
1 lemon/orange	570 ml (1 pt.) water

Method:

Rub the sugar on the thinly pared (discard pith) lemon rind and place in a saucepan, to this add a pinch of cinnamon and a grating of nutmeg and the strained juice of the lemon, then add the ale, water, cloves and spirits. Stir and gently heat until quite hot – avoid *boiling* – serve hot with thin slices of orange or lemon on top.

FEATHERBED PUNCH

Ingredients:

3 glasses red wine	3 dessertspoons honey
1 glass whisky	430 ml (¾ pt.) boiling water

Method:

Place the wine, honey and whisky in serving vessel and add the *boiling* water. Stir and serve. A half hot punch is half hearted, so serve sizzling hot.

GINGER DELIGHT

Ingredients:

2 bottles ginger wine	1 small piece root ginger
55 g (2 oz.) sugar	570 ml (1 pt.) water
2 eggs	1 lemon
4 cloves	

Method:

This is a favourite "non-alcoholic" warmer. Boil the cloves, thinly pared lemon rind and root ginger in 570 ml (1 pt.) of water for 20 minutes. Add the ginger wine, sugar, and strained lemon juice. Heat up this mixture and pour half of it on to the beaten eggs. Whisk thoroughly and add the remainder of the mixture, and whisk once more. Serve hot and frothy.

GLOEGG (Swedish traditional Christmas drink)

Ingredients:

1 bottle red wine	1 stick cinnamon
70 g (2½ oz.) blanched almonds	10 cloves
140 ml (¼ pt.) gin	140 g (5 oz.) seedless raisins

Method:

Place the ingredients, with the exception of the nuts and raisins, in the saucepan and heat to almost boiling point. Then remove the saucepan from the heat and add the nuts and raisins and allow these to soak for a few minutes. Serve hot in small glasses in which a spoon has been placed to enable the guests to fish out and eat the nuts and raisins.

HOT TODDY

Ingredients:

1 bottle medium sweet red wine	85 g (3 oz.) honey
1 small stick of cinnamon	1 lemon

Method:

Put the wine, honey and cinnamon in a saucepan and gently heat and add the thinly pared lemon rind and juice and serve hot.

HOT BLACKCURRANT PUNCH

Ingredients:

1 small tin blackcurrant purée	280 ml (½ pt.) claret type wine
1 lemon	570–700 ml (1–1½ pt.) water
280 ml (½ pt.) sherry type wine	hot
	Sugar to taste

Method:

Place the thinly pared lemon rind (no pith) and lemon juice together with the purée, claret and sherry type wines into a saucepan and heat slowly adding the sugar to suit your taste. Add water and heat up (avoid boiling). Remove rinds and serve in glasses with a slice of lemon.

HOT CUP (Eighteenth Century Classic mull)

Ingredients:

1 bottled red wine	12 lumps of sugar
1 wineglass of brandy	Grated nutmeg
1 wineglass of orange curaçao	570 ml (1 pt.) boiling water
6 cloves	

Method:

Place the sugar, cloves and wine into the saucepan and bring slowly to almost boiling then add the *boiling* water, brandy and curaçao. Pour into glasses and sprinkle with grated nutmeg when serving.

PARTY CHEER

Ingredients:

1 bottled red wine	1 sherry glass liqueur
4 sticks of cinnamon	Sugar to taste
1 glass port wine	

Method:

Most simple to prepare. Just heat the mixture, avoiding boiling, and serve hot.

RUM PUNCH

This makes approximately 570 ml (1 pt.) of punch – just enough to send the pair of you to bed comfortably on Christmas Eve!

Ingredients:
- 3 sherry glasses rum
- 3 sherry glasses white country wine
- 1 sherry glass of ginger wine
- Juice of 1 lemon
- 2 tablespoonsful Demerara sugar
- 1 sliced lemon
- 3 sherry glasses of water

Method:

Put sugar in small mixing bowl with lemon juice, add heated white wine and ginger wine, put in sliced lemon and stir. Now add rum and *boiling* water. Serve hot from bowl.

VIN CHAUD (Hot Wine)

Here it is, simple and cheap!

Ingredients:
- 1 bottle red wine
- 2 oranges
- 1 tablespoonsful sugar
- 280 ml (½ pt.) water
- Grating of nutmeg

Method:

Mix all the ingredients including the thinly pared rinds of the oranges – throw away pith – and place in a saucepan. Heat the mixture until it is very hot, avoid boiling. Pour into china mugs and drink as hot as possible – as should all Punches be drunk.

Quince

Ingredients:
- 24 quinces
- 225 g (½ lb.) raisins
- 1.3 kg (3 lb.) sugar
- 2 lemons
- Yeast and nutrient
- Water to 4.5 litres (1 gal.)

Method:

Grate the quinces as near to the core as possible – a slow job, this – and boil the resultant pulp in the water for 15 minutes; then strain and throw the pulp away. Pour the liquid on to the sugar, and add the chopped raisins and the lemon juice. Stir well. Cool to 20°C (70°F) before adding the yeast and nutrient. Stand the bowl or polythene bucket in a warm place, covered closely with a cloth, for about 10 days, giving the liquor a thorough stirring daily. Then strain into a fermentating jar and fit air-lock. Leave in a temperature of 15–17°C (60–70°F) for about three months, then rack and proceed as usual. N.B. Be careful not to *over*boil the quince pulp or the wine will prove difficult to clear. This can be avoided by adding a tablespoon of Pectolase to the liquid when it has cooled, and delaying the addition of the yeast and nutrient for 24 hours to allow the Pectolase to do its work first.

Quince and Apricot

(A pleasant dessert wine with a heavy bouquet)

Ingredients:

    900 g (2 lb.) (15 approx.) quinces
    450 g (1 lb.) dried apricots (or figs)
    55 g (2 oz.) dried bananas (or 450 g (1 lb.) fresh bananas including skins)
    1.3 kg (3 lb.) sugar (or 1.8 kg (4 lb.) honey)
    15 g (½ oz.) citric acid (or 3 lemons, no pith, in lieu)
    Pectic enzyme
    3 g ($^1/_{10}$ oz.) grape tannin (or 280 ml (½ pt.) strong tea)
    Water to finally make up 4.5 litres (1 gal.) of "must"
    Yeast nutrient and activated wine yeast

Method:

Grate the quinces and simmer the "pulp" for 15 minutes (avoid boiling otherwise the wine may not clear). Place the chopped fruits

"Now that's what I call full bodied, Harry."

and sugar into the initial fermentation vessel, including chopped banana skins, if fresh bananas are used. Pour into this the hot liquor and quince pulp. Stir well with a wooden spoon to dissolve the sugar, etc. When cooled down to 20°C (70°F) add the citric acid, Pectolase, grape tannin and yeast nutrient. Introduce the activated wine yeast and ferment on the "pulp" for 7 days, stirring each day, with a wooden spoon and ensuring the "must" is closely covered. Then strain into the secondary fermentation vessel and leave to ferment under the protection of a fermentation lock, racking as necessary.

Quince and Bilberry

Ingredients:

15 quinces (900 g (2 lb.) approx.)
225 g (½ lb.) dried bilberries (or elderberries)
1.3 kg (3 lb.) sugar (or 1.8 kg (4 lb.) honey)
15 g (½ oz.) citric acid (or 3 lemons, no pith, in lieu)
Pectic enzyme
280 ml (½ pt.) strong tea (or a pinch of grape tannin)
Water to finally make up 4.5 litres (1 gal.) of "must"
Yeast nutrient and activated wine yeast

Method:

Grate the quinces as near to the core as possible and simmer the "pulp" in water for 15 minutes (avoid exceeding this period). Place the dried bilberries and sugar into the initial fermentation vessel and pour into this the hot "pulp" and liquor. Stir well with a wooden spoon to dissolve the sugar, etc. When cooled down to 20°C (70°F) add the citric acid, Pectolase, strong tea and yeast nutrient. Introduce the activated yeast and ferment for 7 days, stirring each day with a wooden spoon. Then strain into the secondary fermentation vessel and leave to ferment under the protection of an air-lock, racking as necessary.

Red-currant

Ingredients:

1.8 kg (4 lb.) red-currants
Water to 4.5 litres (1 gal.)
1 Campden tablet
1.5 kg (3½ lb.) granulated sugar
Yeast and nutrient

Method:

Remove any stems from fruit and wash it well. Press it in a bowl with a wooden spoon. Bring 2 litre (4 pt.) of the water to the boil and mix with the fruit. Crush the Campden tablet and mix with two tablespoons warm water. Add to the fruit. Cover bowl with polythene and leave to stand in a warm place for 24 hours stirring occasionally. Strain mixture through muslin or nylon sieve into polythene bucket. Discard "pulp". Boil remaining water; dissolve sugar in it; pour syrup on to fruit. When the water has cooled slightly, add yeast. Cover bucket with polythene and leave in a warm place for 7 days for the first fermentation. Pour wine into glass jar through funnel; fit cork and lock and leave until fermentation has stopped. Rack wine into bottles.

Red Dock

Ingredients:

450 g (1 lb.) red dock leaves
450 g (1 lb.) raisins (sultanas or currants, etc.)
55 g (2 oz.) dried bananas
1.3 kg (3 lb.) sugar
280 ml (½ pt.) strong tea (or a pinch of grape tannin)
15 g (½ oz.) citric acid (or 3 lemons, no pith, in lieu)
Water to finally make up 4.5 litres (1 gal.) of "must"
Yeast nutrient and activated wine yeast

Method:

Shred the leaves and place these together with the chopped fruits and sugar into the initial fermentation vessel. Pour in the *boiling* water and stir well with a wooden spoon to dissolve the sugar. When cool add the citric acid, strong tea, and yeast nutrient. Introduce the activated wine yeast and ferment on the "pulp" for 7 days, stirring the "must" daily with a wooden spoon and keep it closely covered. Then strain, for secondary fermentation, into the fermentation vessel and fit air-lock. Leave to ferment in the normal way, racking as necessary.

Red Table Wines

RECIPE 1

Ingredients:

4.5 kg (10 lb.) elderberries	Nutrient
4.5 kg (10 lb.) raisins	Beaujolais yeast starter
1.8 kg (4 lb.) sugar	Water to 20 litres (4½ gals.)

Method:

Crush the elderberries and strain off the juice. Leach the "pulp" by adding 4.5 litres (1 gal.) of *boiling* water, stirring for five minutes and then straining off the "pulp". Repeat this treatment with 4.5 litres (1 gal.) of *boiling* water. Add the raisins and nutrients to this elderberry extract followed by another 6.75 litres (1½ gals.) water. When cool add the yeast starter and ferment on the "pulp" for four days. Strain off the "pulp" and press lightly. Add the sugar, stir until completely dissolved and make up the volume to 20 litres (4½ gals.) with water. Thereafter continue as usual with fermenting, racking and bottling.

RECIPE 2

Ingredients:

9 kg (20 lb.) cherries	1.8 kg (4 lb.) sugar
1.8 kg (4 lb.) raisins	Nutrients
1.1 litres (2 pt.) red grape concentrate	Pommard yeast starter
	Water to 20 litres (4½ gals.)

132

Method:

Add *boiling* water to the washed cherries and raisins. Add the nutrients and sugar and stir until dissolved. When cool add the yeast starter. Ferment on the "pulp" until a sample drawn off from the bulk is sufficiently deep in colour. Strain off and press the "pulp" lightly. Add the grape concentrate and make the volume up to 20 litres (4½ gals.) with water. Thereafter proceed as usual.

RECIPE 3

Ingredients:

5.5 kg (12 lb.) elderberries	**Nutrients**
2.2 kg (5 lb.) greengages	**Bordeaux yeast starter**
1.1 litres (2 pt.) red grape	**Water to 20 litres (4½ gals.)**
concentrate	
2.7 kg (6 lb.) sugar	

Method:

Crush the elderberries and strain "pulp" by adding 4.5 litres (1 gal.) *boiling* water, stirring for five minutes then straining off the "pulp". Repeat this procedure with a 4.5 litres (1 gal.) of *boiling* water. Add the stoned greengages, sugar, nutrients and another 4.5 litres (1 gal.) of water to this elderberry extract and stir well until dissolved. When cool add the yeast starter. Ferment on the "pulp" for four days then strain off the "pulp" and press lightly. Add the grape concentrate and make the volume up to 20 litres (4½ gals.) with water. Thereafter proceed as usual.

RECIPE 4

Ingredients:

5.5 kg (12 lb.) bilberries	**Nutrients**
4.5 kg (10 lb.) peaches	**Pommard yeast starter**
1.1 litres (2 pt.) red grape	**Water to 20 litres (4½ gals.)**
concentrate	
2.7 kg (6 lb.) sugar	

Method:

Crush the bilberries and add the stoned peaches. Add 12 litres (2½ gals.) *boiling* water, sugar and nutrients and stir until dissolved. When cool add the yeast starter. Ferment on the "pulp" until a satisfactory depth of colour is attained then strain off the "pulp" and press lightly. Add the grape concentrate and sufficient water to make the volume up to 20 litres (4½ gals.). Thereafter proceed as usual.

RECIPE 5

Ingredients:

11 kg (25 lb.) dessert apples	**Nutrients**
5.5 kg (12 lb.) elderberries	**Pommard yeast starter**
1.1 litres (2 pt.) red grape concentrate	**Water to 20 litres (4½ gals.)**
2.25 kg (5 lb.) sugar	

Method:

Crush the elderberries and strain off the juice. Add 4.5 litres (1 gal.) *boiling* water to the pulp, stir for five minutes then strain off the "pulp". Repeat this treatment with a further 4.5 litres (1 gal.) of boiling water. Add the elderberry juice and hot extracts to the washed sliced apples. Dissolve the sugar and nutrients in this solution. When cool add the yeast starter. Ferment on the "pulp" for seven days then strain off the "pulp" and press lightly. Add the grape concentrate and sufficient water to make the volume up to 20 litres (4½ gals.). Thereafter proceed as usual.

RECIPE 6

Ingredients:

11 kg (25 lb.) plums (red or blue)	**900 g (2 lb.) honey**
1.8 kg (4 lb.) raisins	**Nutrients**
20 litres (4 pt.) red grape concentrate	**Pommard yeast starter**
	Water to 20 litres (4½ gals.)
	30 g (1 oz.) pectinol

Method:

Wash and stone the plums and add the raisins and honey. Add 13.5 litres (3 gals.) *boiling* water and the nutrients. When cool add the pectinol and yeast starter. Ferment on the "pulp" for five to six days then strain off the "pulp" and press lightly. Add the red grape concentrate and sufficient water to make the volume up to 20 litres (4½ gals.) . Thereafter proceed as usual.

RECIPE 7

Ingredients:

6.8 kg (15 lb.) elderberries **Nutrients**
2.7 kg (6 lb.) bananas **Rhone or Burgundy yeast**
1.1 litres (2 pt.) red grape **starter**
  concentrate **Water to 20 litres (4½ gals.)**
4 kg (9 lb.) sugar

Method:

Crush the elderberries and strain off the juice. Peel the bananas and cut into slices (discarding the skins). Boil the slices in 4.5 litres (1 gal.) water for half an hour then strain the hot liquor over the elderberry "pulp". Stir for five minutes then strain off the "pulp". Repeat this treatment with another 4.5 litres (1 gal.) *boiling* water. Dissolve the sugar and nutrients in the combined extracts. When cool add the grape concentrate and make up the volume to 16 litres (3½ gals.) with water. Add the yeast starter. When the first violent fermentation has abated top up to 20 litres (4½ gals.) with water. Thereafter proceed as usual.

Rhubarb

Rhubarb picked mid-May is best for winemaking

Ingredients:

2.25 kg (5 lb.) rhubarb stalks
1.5 kg (3½ lb.) preserving sugar
Yeast
Juice of 2 lemons

4.5 litres (1 gal.) water
Precipitated chalk
Yeast nutrient

Method:

Wipe the rhubarb clean, but do not peel, and chop into short lengths. Pour the boiling water over it, allow it to become cold, then strain off the liquor and add to it the juice pressed from the stalks. Add the precipitated chalk and the juice will fizz as the acid is reduced. Then put in the sugar, stirring well until all is dissolved, add the juice pressed out of two large lemons, and put in the yeast. Put into fermentation vessel and fit air-lock, keeping 140 ml (½ pt.) or so separately in a bottle plugged with cotton wool for "topping up" when the ferment quietens. Leave until the wine clears, then siphon off for the first time. If you wish to remove all colour add half a dozen clean, broken eggshells.

Rhubarb and Centaury

Ingredients:

1.8 kg (4 lb.) rhubarb
1 packet centaury herb
   or 225 g (½ lb.) fresh herb (the whole herb is used)
450 g (1 lb.) raisins (or other dried fruit)
1.5 kg (3½ lb.) sugar
280 ml (½ pt.) strong tea (or a pinch of grape tannin)
15 g (½ oz.) citric acid (or 3 lemons, no pith, in lieu)
Sufficient water to finally produce 4.5 litres (1 gal.) "must"
Yeast nutrient and activated wine yeast

Method:

Having extracted the rhubarb juice by the cold water method, place the herb in a boiler and simmer in the remainder of the water cutting off the heat at *boiling* point. Leave to infuse for three hours. Place the chopped fruit and sugar in the initial fermentation vessel. Bring the herb liquor up to *boiling* point, then strain into fermentation vessel, stirring to dissolve the sugar. When cool add the rhubarb juice, strong tea, citric acid, yeast nutrient and introduce the activated wine yeast. Ferment, closely covered for 7 days, then siphon into fermentation bottle. Fit air-lock and leave to ferment in normal way, racking as necessary. The herb is a bitter tonic and produces an "appetiser" type wine.

Rhubarb and Bilberry

Ingredients:

1.8 kg (4 lb.) rhubarb
225 g (½ lb.) dried bilberries or elderberries (110 g of each, together may also be used)
450 g (1 lb.) raisins or other dried fruit
1.3 kg (3 lb.) sugar
280 ml (½ pt.) strong tea (or a pinch of grape tannin)
15 g (½ oz.) citric acid
Sufficient water to finally produce 4.5 litres (1 gal.) of "must"
Yeast nutrient and activated wine yeast

Method:

Using half the water, prepare the rhubarb by the cold water method removing excess oxalic acid by using precipitated chalk – extraction by hot water may cause jellification; place the chopped raisins and other fruits together with the sugar in the initial fermentation vessel and pour over the remainder of the water, *boiling* hot. Stir well to dissolve the sugar. When cool add the prepared rhubarb juice, strong tea, citric acid, yeast nutrient and introduce the activated wine yeast. Ferment, closely covered, for 7 days, then strain into fermentation bottle. Fit air-lock and leave to ferment in the normal way, racking as necessary.

Rhubarb and Chervil Root

Ingredients:

1.3–1.8 kg (3–4 lb.) rhubarb
900 g (2 lb.) chervil root (carrots may be substituted)
1.5 kg (3½ lb.) sugar
140 ml (¼ pt.) strong tea (or a pinch of grape tannin)
15 g (½ oz.) citric acid (or 3 lemons, no pith, in lieu)
Sufficient water to finally produce 4.5 litres (1 gal.) "must"
Yeast nutrient and activated wine yeast

Method:

Extract the rhubarb juice by the cold water method. Boil the chervil roots or carrots until slightly tender in the remainder of the water. Place the sugar in the initial crock bowl and strain in the root juice, and stir to dissolve the sugar. When cool add the citric acid, strong tea, rhubarb juice, yeast nutrient and introduce the activated wine yeast. Keep closely covered and ferment for 48 hours. Strain into fermentation bottle. Fit air-lock and leave to ferment in the normal way, racking in due course. Chervil roots can be cooked and served the same way as carrots. Roots for storing should be lifted in August.

Rhubarb and Chervil Flower

Ingredients:

1.3–1.8 kg (3–4 lb.) rhubarb
1.1 litres (2 pt.) chervil flower heads (or flower heads and leaves combined). (The root if lifted can be cooked and eaten as carrots)
1.5 kg (3½ lb.) sugar
280 ml (½ pt.) strong tea (or a pinch of grape tannin)
15 g (½ oz.) citric acid (or 3 lemons, no pith, in lieu)
Sufficient water to finally produce 4.5 litres (1 gal.) of "must"
Yeast nutrient and activated wine yeast

"A Campden tablet, please, waiter"

Method:

Prepare the rhubarb juice by the cold water method. Infuse the flower heads/leaves, etc., by simmering in remainder of the water cutting off heat at boiling point. Leave to infuse for three hours, then bring back to boiling point and strain on to sugar in initial fermentation vessel. Stir well to dissolve sugar and when cool add the rhubarb juice, strong tea, citric acid, yeast nutrient and activated wine yeast. Ferment, closely covered for 48 hours, then transfer to fermentation jars. Fit air-lock and leave to ferment in the normal way, racking as necessary. This herb has a flavour of caraway and anise and blends well with the other ingredients.

Rhubarb and Clover

Ingredients:

1.3–1.8 kg (3–4 lb.) rhubarb
335 g (¾ lb.) purple clover blossom (3.5 litres (¾ gal.) flower heads)
450 g (1 lb.) raisins (or other dried fruit)
15 g (2 oz.) citric acid (or 3 lemons, no pith, in lieu)
280 ml (½ pt.) strong tea (or a pinch of grape tannin)
1.3 kg (3 lb.) sugar
Sufficient water to finally produce 4.5 litres (1 gal.) of "must"
Yeast nutrient and activated wine yeast

Method:

Wipe the rhubarb clean with a damp cloth. Do not peel, then cut into lengths and crush with a mallet, or pulper, or put through a domestic wringer! (enclosing the rhubarb in a muslin cloth) to extract as much juice as possible. Leave the juice and "pulp" in the crock and add one Campden tablet, then add 2 litres (½ gal.) of cold water and leave to this to soak, closely covered, for three days, stirring several times each day. Strain into fermentation jar, then add 15 g (½ oz.) of precipitated chalk (obtainable from the chemist). Fit air-lock and leave for 24 hours, then siphon into a clean jar, being most careful not to disturb residue from the bottom of the jar. When this has been completed place the blossoms (flower heads), the chopped raisins and sugar into the initial fermentation vessel and pour in 2 litres (½ gal.) *boiling* water and stir to dissolve the sugar. When cool add the treated rhubarb juice, citric acid, strong tea, yeast nutrient and lastly the activated wine yeast. Leave to ferment with the solids, for seven days, closely covered. Strain into fermentation jar. Fit air-lock and leave to ferment in the normal way, racking as necessary.

Rhubarb and Ginger

Ingredients:
    1.8 kg (4 lb.) rhubarb
    55 g (2 oz.) root ginger (or powdered ginger)
    900 g (1 lb.) raisins (or other dried fruit)
    225 g (½ lb.) oak leaves (1 litre (2 qt.)) (or 225 g (½ lb.) tips of young blackberry shoots)
    1.3 kg (3 lb.) sugar
    280 ml (½ pt.) strong tea (or a pinch of grape tannin)
    15 g (½ oz.) citric acid (or 3 lemons, no pith, in lieu)
    Sufficient water to finally produce 4.5 litres (1 gal.) of "must"
    Yeast nutrient and activated wine yeast

Method:
Use cold water extraction method to prepare the rhubarb juice. Place the washed shoots or leaves in the boiler and simmer in the remainder of the water, cutting off heat when at *boiling* point. Leave to infuse for three hours, then bring back to *boiling* point. Place the chopped fruit, crushed ginger and sugar into initial fermentation vessel and pour in the strained extract of the leaves or shoots. Stir well to dissolve the sugar. When cool add the rhubarb juice, strong tea, citric acid, yeast nutrient and introduce the activated wine yeast. Leave closely covered for 7 days, then siphon in fermentation jar. Fit air-lock, and leave to ferment in normal way, racking as necessary.

141

Rhubarb and Hawthorn Blossom

Ingredients:
   1.3–1.8 kg (3–4 lb.) rhubarb
   110 g (¼ lb.) hawthorn blossom (May blossom) (or 1 litre (1 qt.)
      blossom)
   55 g (2 oz.) dried bananas
   1.5 kg (3½ lb.) sugar
   280 ml (½ pt.) strong tea (or a pinch of grape tannin)
   15 g (½ oz.) citric acid (or 3 lemons, no pith, in lieu)
   Sufficient water to finally produce 4.5 litres (1 gal.) of "must"
   Yeast nutrient and activated wine yeast

Method:
Prepare the rhubarb by the cold water extraction method. Place the blossoms fruit and sugar in the initial fermentation vessel and pour in the remainder of the water *boiling* hot, then stir to dissolve the sugar. When cool, add the rhubarb juice, strong tea, citric acid, yeast nutrient and introduce the activated wine yeast. Leave, closely covered, to ferment for seven days, then strain into fermentation jar. Fit air-lock and leave to ferment in the normal way, racking as necessary.

Rhubarb and Nettle

Ingredients:
   1.3–1.8 kg (3–4 lb.) rhubarb
   225 g (½ lb.) young nettle tops (2 litres (2 qt.))
   110 g (¼ lb.) dried rose-hips/shells
   450 g (1 lb.) raisins (or other dried fruit)
   1.3 kg (3 lb.) sugar
   280 ml (½ pt.) strong tea (or a pinch of grape tannin)
   15 g (½ oz.) citric acid (or 3 lemons, no pith, in lieu)
   Sufficient water to finally produce 4.5 litres (1 gal.) of "must"
   Yeast nutrient and activated wine yeast

Method:

Prepare the rhubarb by the cold water extraction method. Wash and drain the young nettle tops and simmer these in the remainder of the water. Bring the water to *boiling* point then cut off heat and leave to soak for three hours and re-heat to almost boiling point. Place the rose-hips, chopped dried fruit and sugar into the initial fermentation vessel and strain in the hot nettle extract. Stir well to dissolve the sugar. When cool add the rhubarb juice, strong tea, citric acid, yeast nutrient and lastly the activated wine yeast. Leave closely covered for 7 days then siphon into fermentation jar. Fit air-lock and leave to ferment in normal way, racking as necessary. In the initial stages of fermentation the nettle gives off a very strong odour – this need cause no concern as it does not persist.

Rhubarb and Spruce

Ingredients:

1.8 kg (4 lb.) rhubarb
10 g (¼ oz.) essence spruce (or a T. Noirot Extract to your own choice)
1.8 kg (4 lb.) sugar
280 ml (½ pt.) strong tea (or a pinch of grape tannin)
15 g (½ oz.) citric acid (or 3 lemons, no pith, in lieu)
Sufficient water to finally produce 4.5 litres (1 gal.) of "must"
Yeast nutrient and activated wine yeast

Method:

Using half the water, prepare the rhubarb by the cold water method, sing precipitated chalk, which costs a few pence from any chemists store. Use of hot water may cause jellification. Heat the remainder of the water and place the sugar in the initial fermentation vessel and pour in the hot water. Stir to dissolve the sugar. When cool add the rhubarb juice, strong tea, citric acid and nutrient, and then introduce the activated wine yeast. Ferment, closely covered, for two days, then transfer to fermentation bottles. Add the essence of extract and fit air-lock. Leave to ferment in the normal way, racking later as necessary.

Rice

Ingredients:

450 g (1 lb.) coarsely crushed rice
450 g (1 lb.) minced raisins
1.3 kg (3 lb.) sugar

Water to 4.5 litres (1 gal.)
Yeast and nutrient
2 lemons

Method:

Pour *boiling* water on to the rice, sugar, raisins and thinly peeled skin of the lemon. Stir well and cover. When cool 20°C (70°F) add the lemon juice, nutrient and yeast, and ferment all together for one week, stirring twice daily and keeping the crock or polythene bucket well covered. Strain into fermenting jar (without pressing) and ferment out. Rack when clear, and again two months later into clean bottles.

Rose-hip

Ingredients:

1.1 kg (2½ lb.) fresh rose-hips
(or 225 g (6–8 oz.) bottle
rose-hip syrup
1 lemon

1.3 kg (3 lb.) sugar
Pectic enzyme
Water to 4.5 litres (1 gal.)
Yeast and yeast nutrient

Method:

The easiest way to crush the rose-hips is to run them through an ordinary domestic mincer with the outer cutting disc removed. The inner disc has holes just too small to allow them to pass freely and they are neatly crushed in the process (crushing them with a mallet or rolling pin, as sometimes recommended, is a tedious and sticky business). Pour over them the water, *boiling*. Allow to cool to 20°C (70°F) then add the Pectolase and stir well in. Leave for 24 hours, covered with a cloth, then add the sugar, stirring well to dissolve it, a general purpose wine yeast, nutrient, and the juice of the lemon. Keep in a warm place, about 20°C (70°F) closely covered, for five or six days, stirring vigorouslyonce a day. By then the fermentation will have quietened a little, so strain the liquor into a fermentation jar and fit an air-lock. Rack and bottle in the usual way. This is a strong-flavoured wine, high in alcohol, and some may prefer to sweeten it a little after it is made.

Rose-Hip (dried)

Ingredients:

375 g (13 oz.) dried rose-hips
1.1 kg (2½ lb.) sugar
Juice of 1 lemon

Tokay yeast and yeast
  nutrient
Water to 4.5 litres (1 gal.)

Method:

Dried rose-hips can now be purchased in this country and one can thus avoid the tedious business of picking fresh hips. The dried ones make a wine fully as good, and rose-hip wine *is* good, indeed the Germans hold that it is second only to the grape for winemaking. With the dried rose-hips, which have been largely dehydrated, and therefoe weigh less, a smaller quantity is required than when one uses the fresh fruit. Prepare your yeast starter two days before making the wine and soak the rose-hips overnight in 570 ml (1 pt.) of water. Mince your rose-hips through an ordinary domestic mincer with the outer cutting disc removed and put into a bowl with the sugar and lemon juice. Pour over them the water, *boiling*. Stir well to dissolve the sugar. When the mixture has cooled to 20°C (70°F) add your fermenting Tokaier yeast. Cover closely with a polythene sheet secured by elastic and stand in a warm place (about 20°C (70°F) but stir daily. After 7 days, strain into a fermentation jar, topping up with cold boiled water to the bottom of the neck if necessary, and fit air-lock. When the wine clears rack into a clean jar and refit lock. Leave for a further three months, then rack into clean bottle and cork down.

Rose-hip and Fig

(A dry white wine)

This is an adaptation of a Vierka recipe, using rose-hip syrup instead of rose-hip syrup instead of rose-hip shells. The original recipe is to produce a mock Tokay, the popular Hungarian wine, but this version produced a dry white wine almost identical to a good Liebfraumilch.

   1 small bottle of Delrosa rose-hip syrup
   110 g (4 oz.) figs
   1 teaspoon citric acid
   1.5 kg (3½ lb.) sugar
   5 litres (9 pt.) water
   1 Tokay yeast; nutrient

Method:

Wash the figs well, chop well, and put them in a polythene bucket with the sugar. Pour in 4.5 litres (1 gal.) of *boiling* water. Allow to cool, then add citric acid, yeast and nutrient, cover closely and ferment for about a week, closely covered. Strain through muslin or sieve into a fermentation jar, adding the rose-hip syrup dissolved in any convenient amount of warm "must", a little at a time. Fit air-lock and ferment out in a warm place (about four to five weeks).

Rosemary and Carrot

Ingredients:

   55 g (2 oz.) packet of dried rosemary herb or 450 g (1 lb.) fresh herb
      (Rosemary Officinalis)
   1.8 kg (4 lb.) old carrots
   450 g (1 lb.) figs or raisins
   1.1 kg (2½ lb.) sugar
   Juice of 2 lemons
   3 g (¹/₁₀ oz.) grape tannin
   Water to finally make up 4.5 litres (1 gal.) of "must"
   Yeast nutrient and activated wine yeast

146

Method:

Scrub the carrots and chop them up, put them in the water and bring to the boil. Simmer until tender. Place the chopped fruit, sugar and herb into the initial fermentation vessel and strain into this the hot carrot liquor (the carrots may be eaten) and stir well to dissolve the sugar, etc. When cool (20°C, 70°F) add the citric acid and yeast nutrient. Introduce the activated yeast and ferment for 7 days stirring every day with a wooden spoon. Then strain into secondary fermentation vessel and leave to ferment under the protection of an air-lock, racking as necessary.

Rose Petal and Concentrate

Ingredients:

2 litres (2 qt.) strongly scented petals
570 ml (1 pt.) grape concentrate
15 g (½ oz.) citric acid (or 2 lemons, no pith, in lieu)
280 ml (½ pt.) strong tea (or 3 g ¹/₁₀ oz. grape tannin)
1.3 kg (3 lb.) sugar (1.1 kg (2½ lb.) of grape concentrate if used)
Yeast nutrient and activated wine yeast
Water: sufficient to finally produce 4.5 litres (1 gal.) of "must"

Method:

Use any rose petals – different varieties will produce a wine of differing bouquet. Place the petals in the initial fermentation vessel and pour over half of the water, *boiling* hot, cover securely and leave to infuse for two to three days, stirring daily. Then strain and place the rose scented extract back in the initial fermentation vessel and add the sugar. Pour over this the remainder of the water, *boiling* hot, and stir well to dissolve the sugar. When cool add the concentrate, acid, tannin, nutrient, and introduce the activated wine yeast. Cover well and leave to ferment three days, then transfer to fermentation bottles and fit air-lock. Leave to ferment in the normal way, racking as necessary.

Variations:

1. Use 1.8 kg (4 lb.) honey in lieu of sugar.
2. Or add, instead of concentrate, a small bottle of blackcurrant juice or fresh juice from soft fruits, such as raspberries, etc.

Rose Petal and Peach

Ingredients:

2 litres (2 qt.) rose petals (strongly scented are preferred)
1.1 kg (2½ lb.) peaches (or 450 g (1 lb.) dried peaches)
1.3 kg (3 lb.) sugar
1 level teaspoon citric acid (or 2 lemons, no pith, in lieu)
280 ml (½ pt.) strong tea (or a pinch of grape tannin)
Water to finally make 4.5 litres (1 gal.) of "must"
Yeast nutrient and activated wine yeast

Method:

Place the rose petals, stoned peaches (chop up the dried ones) and sugar into the initial fermentation vessel. Pour in the *boiling* water and stir well with a wooden spoon until the sugar is dissolved. When cool add the citric acid, strong tea and yeast nutrient. Introduce the activated wine yeast and ferment on the "pulp" for 7 days, stirring the "must" daily with a wooden spoon and keep it closely covered. Then strain, for secondary fermentation, into a fermentation vessel and fit air-lock. Leave to ferment in the normal way, racking as necessary.

Rowanberry

Ingredients:

2 litres (2 qt.) rowanberries   15 g (½ oz.) yeast
4.5 litres (1 gal.) water   2 tablespoons raisins (heaped)
1.3 kg (3 lb.) sugar   Yeast and nutrient
500 g (1 lb.) wheat

Method:

This makes an excellent medium-sweet table wine, but if you wish to make a dry one cut the sugar to 1.1 kg (2½ lb.). Pour the *boiling* water over the rowanberries, and let them stand for five days, stirring and mashing with the hand daily. Then strain the liquid on to the sugar, chopped raisins, and wheat, and stir well to

"I don't feel too happy about this Judge"

dissolve the sugar. Add the yeast and nutrient (a general purpose) wine yeast starter or a level teaspoon of granulated yeast, and stand in a warm place, closely covered, for a further 7 days. Then strain into fermenting jar, fit air-lock, and leave until fermentation is finished and wine is clear. Then rack into clean jar. Bottle after a further three months.

Sage

Ingredients:

3.6 kg (8 lb.) stoned raisins
450 g (1 lb.) barley (if desired, it will lend "body" to the wine)
1.3 kg (3 lb.) sage leaves
2 lemons
Yeast and nutrient
4.5 litres (1 gal.) water

Method:

Pour the *boiling* water on to the minced raisins and barley and add the chopped leaves of the red sage. Allow to cool and then add the juice of the two lemons and the yeast (a prepared wine yeast or a level teaspoonful of granulated yeast). Keep covered, in a warm place, for seven days, stirring daily, then strain into a fermentation vessel with an air-lock and ferment in the usual way. Alternatively, and more cheaply, the wine can be made by substituting 450 g (1 lb.) raisins and 1.1 kg (2½ lb.) sugar for the 3.6 kg (8 lb.) of raisins.

150

Sage and Parsley

Ingredients:

450 g (1 lb.) fresh parsley (or 55 g (2 oz.) dried parsley)
450 g (1 lb.) sage (or 55 g (2 oz.) dried red sage)
450 g (1 lb.) raisins (or sultanas, peaches, apricots, etc.)
55 g (2 oz.) dried bananas (450 g (1 lb.) fresh bananas including skins)
1.3 kg (3 lb.) sugar (or 1.8 kg (4 lb.) honey)
10 g (¼ oz.) citric acid
1 tablespoon strong tea
Water to finally make up 4.5 litres (1 gal.) of "must"
Yeast and nutrient and activated wine yeast

Method:

Chop up the parsley, sage, raisins and bananas. Place these into the initial fermentation vessel together with the sugar. Pour in the *boiling* water and stir with a wooden spoon to dissolve the sugar. When cool add the citric acid, strong tea, and yeast nutrient. Introduce the activated wine yeast and ferment on the "pulp" for 7 days, stirring the "must" with a wooden spoon daily; otherwise keep it closely covered. Then strain, for secondary fermentation into fermentation vessel, and fit air-lock. Leave to ferment in the normal way, racking as necessary.

Sarsaparilla

Ingredients:

450 g (1 lb.) Sarsaparilla leaves   **2 lemons (or citric acid)**
225 g (½ lb.) chopped raisins   **Yeast nutrient**
1.3 kg (3 lb.) sugar   **Yeast (selected wine)**
    Water to 4.5 litres (1 gal.)

Method:

Pour the *boiling* water over the sarsaparilla leaves, chopped raisins and sugar. When cool add lemon juice or citric acid and the juice from the boiled lemon peel (no pith). Stir in yeast nutrient and activated wine yeast and ferment on the solids for six days, stirring daily. Then strain in fermentation glass jar. Fit air-lock and ferment in normal way.

Note: The sarsaparilla leaves are stocked by most herbalists and wine supplies firms.

Sloe

Ingredients:

1.3 kg (3 lb.) sloes (as ripe as possible)
1.3 kg (3 lb.) sugar
4.5 litres (1 gal.) water
Burgundy yeast and nutrient

Method:

Bring the water to the boil and pour it over the sloes, crushing and breaking them as much as possible, then dissolve 900 g (2 lb.) of sugar in the liquid. Allow the mixture to cool to 20°C (70°F), before adding yeast starter (a Burgundy or Port yeast is excellent, failing that a general purpose yeast) and some yeast nutrient. Put the bowl or polythene bucket in a warm place (about 20°C, 70°F) and cover closely; ferment thus for about five days, stirring well each day. Strain, add the remaining 450 g (1 lb.) of sugar to the juice, and pour into fermenting jar, to the bottom of the neck. Top up with a little cold boiled water if necessary. After about three months (temperature preferably 15–17°C (60–65°F) there will be a yeast deposit, so rack into a clear jar and refit trap. Leave until wine is really clear, then rack into clean bottles and cork down.

Sloe and Apricot

Ingredients:

900 g (2 lb.) sloes
450 g (1 lb.) dried apricots (or figs)
55 g (2 oz.) dried rose-hips or rose-hip shells
225 g (½ lb.) raisins or sultanas
1.3 kg (3 lb.) sugar
Pectic enzyme
Juice of 2 lemons
140 ml (¼ pt.) strong tea
Water to make up finally 4.5 litres (1 gal.) of "must"
Yeast nutrient and activated wine yeast

Method:

Break open the sloes and place together with the chopped dried fruits, hips and sugar into the initial fermentation vessel. Pour in the *boiling* water and stir well with a wooden spoon to dissolve the sugar and mash the fruits. When cooled down to 20°C (70°F) add the citric acid, Pectolase, strong tea and yeast nutrient. Introduce the activated wine yeast and ferment on the "pulp" for 7 days, stirring each day with a wooden spoon and ensuring the "must" is closely covered. Then strain into the secondary fermentation vessel, and leave to ferment under the protection of an air-lock, racking as necessary.

Strawberry and Red-currant

Ingredients:

1.3 kg (3 lb.) strawberries
450 g (1 lb.) red-currants (or white-currants)
55 g (2 oz.) dried bananas (or 85 g (3 oz.) dried rose-hips/shells)
15 g (½ oz.) citric acid (or 3 lemons, no pith, in lieu)
280 ml (½ pt.) strong tea (or 3 g $^{1}/_{10}$ oz.) grape tannin)
15 g (½ oz.) Pectolase
25 g (¾ oz.) glycerine (B.P. quality)
1.3 kg (3 lb.) sugar (or 1.8 kg (4 lb.) honey)
Yeast nutrient and selected wine yeast
Water: sufficient to finally produce 4.5 litres (1 gal.) of "must"

Method:

Place the strawberries and red-currants in the initial fermentation vessel and macerage these with a wooden spoon, add the dried fruit and sugar. Pour over these the *boiling* water and stir well to dissolve the sugar. When cool add the acid, tannin, Pectolase, yeast nutrient and introduce the activated wine yeast. Secure well and leave to ferment for 7 days, then strain into fermentation bottles, add the glycerine and fit air-lock. Leave to ferment in normal way, racking as necessary. Avoid mouldy, damaged or overripe fruit.

Variations:

1. Use 225 g (½ lb.) malt extract in lieu of dried bananas.
2. A bottle of Ribena blackcurrant juice (this should be added when the original "must" is cool).

Tea

Ingredients:

2 litres (4 pt.) tea (saved left-overs)	**225 g (½ lb.) raisins (large and chopped)**
675 g (1½ lb.) sugar	**1 teaspoonful granulated yeast**
2 lemons	

Method:

The key to this most useful, easy-to-make wine is 165 g (6 oz.) of sugar to every 570 ml (pt.) of tea, as you can see from the above. Add the tea which can be saved a little at a time until you have the required quantity, to the sugar and lemon juice and stir until dissolved. Pour into fermenting jar with yeast, nutrient, and chopped raisins, work out, and rack off when clear. A dry wine of a golden colour, and of not too strong a flavour. Excellent for blending purposes.

Turnips

Ingredients:

1.8 kg (4 lb.) turnips	1 orange
1.3 kg (3 lb.) sugar	Yeast and yeast nutrient
1 lemon	4.5 litres (1 gal.) water

Method:

Scrub the roots well – it is not necessary to peel them – and cut them into slices. Put them into a large saucepan or boiler in as much of the water as possible (leaving the remainder of the 4.5 litres (1 gal.) to one side) bring to the boil, and simmer until the turnips are tender. Do not, however, allow them to go mushy or the wine may not clear. Strain off the liquor on to the remaining water, return it to the boiler, and add the sliced fruit and sugar. Simmer for half an hour, stirring well for the first few minutes, then strain through a nylon sieve or two thicknesses of muslin into a bowl or jar, and make it up to 4.5 litres (1 gal.) once more. Allow the liquor to cool to 20°C (70°F), then add your yeast (a wine yeast or 25 g (¾ oz.) baker's yeast) and nutrient, and stir well. Cover bowl closely and leave for four days in a warm place (about 20°C, 70°F), then lower temperature and after three months the wine should be clearing and can be racked, or siphoned into a clean bottle, leaving the sediment behind. Again fit an air-lock. Leave for a further three months; then rack it again, this time into the wine bottles and cork securely.

Veitchberry

Ingredients:

1.8 kg (4 lb.) veitchberries (a hybrid between a large blackberry and raspberry)
570 ml (1 pt.) home-made or commercial cider
1.3 kg (3 lb.) sugar
Juice of 1 large lemon
10 g (¼ oz.) Pectolase
Water to finally make up 4.5 litres (1 gal.) of "must"
Yeast nutrient and activated wine yeast

Method:

Place the berries into the initial fermentation vessel and add the sugar. Pour in the *boiling* water. Macerate and stir well with a wooden spoon to break up the berries and to dissolve the sugar. When cool add the cider, lemon juice, Pectolase and yeast nutrient. Introduce the activated wine yeast and ferment on the "pulp" for 7 days, stirring the "must" daily with a wooden spoon, and keep it closely covered. Then strain, for secondary fermentation, into fermentation vessel and fit air-lock. Leave it to ferment in the normal way, racking as necessary in due course. (Blackberries and raspberries may be used in lieu of veitchberries.)

Red Wine

(Vin Ordinaire)

Ingredients:

> **450 g (1 lb.) fresh elderberries (or 110 g (¼ lb.) dried)**
> **450 g (1 lb.) raisins (or 140 ml (¼ pt.) red grape concentrate)**
> **675 g (1½ lb.) sugar**
> **1 teaspoon Pectolase or equivalent**
> **Burgundy yeast and nutrient**
> **2 lemons (or 10 g (¼ oz.) citric acid)**
> **Water to 4.5 litres (1 gal.)**

Method:

The ingredients are crushed and placed in a bucket and *boiling* water is poured over them. The water level is brought up to 4.5 litres (1 gal.) and when cool the yeast starter and Pectolase are added. The "pulp" is strained off after four days and thereafter fermentation continues in a fermentation jar. Rack when all sugar has been used up (generally within a month) and allow to clear. This wine will also improve rapidly if matured in cask for a few months, but in any case can be drunk at six to nine months as a rough table wine similar to the carafe wines of France.

White Wine

(Vin Ordinaire)

Ingredients:

> 140 ml (¼ pt.) canned orange juice
> 280 ml (½ pt.) canned pineapple juice
> 900 g (2 lb.) sugar
> Pectic enzyme
> Bordeaux yeast
> Water to 4.5 litres (1 gal.)

Method:

The sugar is poured into a fermentation jar, the juices and nutrients, etc., are added and the jar is topped up to the shoulder with cold water. Vigorous stirring will dissolve the sugar and the yeast starter and Pectolase are added immediately. This wine will ferment out to dryness in about three to four weeks at 20°C (70°F). At the end of this time two Campden tablets should be added and the wine racked a week later. After three to four months the wine is brilliantly clear and is drinkable as a rough white wine but is much improved if cask matured for two months.

Vine Prunings

In the summer you are pruning your vines to keep them under control – each shoot should be pinched out leaving one leaf beyond each cluster of grape flowers and as the summer goes on you are likely to have plenty of prunings. Do not waste these, for they will make excellent wine. Here is a good recipe for a wine from a white grape vine such as Seyve Villard

Ingredients:

> 3 litres (6 pt.) boiling water
> 1.8–2.2 kg (4–5 lb.) leaves and tendrils
> 1.3 kg (3 lb.) sugar
>
> Juice of 1 lemon
> Yeast and nutrient

Method:

Chop the leaves, stems and tendrils – use a pair of secateurs – put them into a receptacle and pour over them the *boiling* water. Let this stand for 48 hours, but turn occasionally to submerge top leaves and keep prunings well under water (there will be only just enough water). Keep closely covered. Pour off liquid and press out leaves; if you have no press wring them in your hands. Wash the leaves with 570 ml (1 pt.) of water and press again. Dissolve the sugar in the liquid, add the yeast, yeast nutrient and acid, pour into fermenting jar, and make up to 4.5 litres (1 gal.) with water. Fit air-lock. Ferment right out in the usual way and siphon off when clear.

Wheat

Ingredients:

570 ml (1 pt.) wheat	**1.5 kg (3½ lb.) Demerara sugar**
900 g (2 lb.) raisins	**Water to 4.5 litres (1 gal.)**
2 lemons	**Yeast and nutrient**
1 orange	

Method:

Put the wheat (crushed through a mincer) and chopped raisins into crock, together with the lemon rinds (no white pith), the fruit juice, and the sugar. Cover with *boiling* water and leave till cool, stirring at intervals. Add yeast and leave well covered in a warm place until vigorous fermentation has ceased. Strain into a fermenting jar and fit air-lock, keep for about four months, and then siphon off into clean bottles. Leave at least six months before drinking. This is an excellent full-bodied sweet wine.

White-currant

Ingredients:

**1.8 kg (4 lb.) white-currants (or white elderberries when
    available)**
450 g (1 lb.) raisins (or other dried fruit)
55 g (2 oz.) dried bananas
1.3 kg (3 lb.) sugar
15 g (½ oz.) citric acid (or 3 lemons, no pith, in lieu)
280 ml (½ pt.) strong tea (or a pinch of grape tannin)
Pectic enzyme
Water to finally make up 4.5 litres (1 gal.) of "must"
Yeast nutrient and activated wine yeast

Method:

Place the fruits and sugar into the initial fermentation vessel and
pour in the *boiling* water. Macerate and stir well with a wooden
spoon to break up the fruits and to dissolve the sugar. When cool
add the citric acid, strong tea, Pectolase and yeast nutrient.
Introduce the activated wine yeast and ferment on the "pulp" for 7
days, stirring the "must" daily with a wooden spoon and keep it
closely covered. Then strain, for secondary fermentation, into a
fermentation vessel and fit air-lock. Leave to ferment in the normal
way, racking as necessary.

Woodruff

A good old-fashioned favourite. The woodruff is found in woods
and shady places especially amongst the leaf mould of beech
woods. It flowers in May and June.

Ingredients:

**4.5 litres (1 gal.) woodruff
    flowers and leaves (no
    stalks)**
1.5 kg (3½ lb.) sugar
280 ml (½ pt.) cold tea

**2 lemons (or 10 g (¼ oz.) citric
    acid)**
450 g (1 lb.) barley (crushed)
Water to 4.5 litres (1 gal.)
Activated yeast and nutrient

Method:

Soak and crush the barley and place in fermentation jar with grated lemon rinds (no white pith) and the florets and bruised leaves of the woodruff together with the sugar. Pour in the boiling water, stir to dissolve the sugar and leave to cool. Add the cold tea, lemon juice or citric acid, activated yeast and nutrient. Ferment and rack in the usual way.

Variations may be made by adding chopped raisins (scalded) grape concentrate, with adjustment to sugar used.

"I'd like to try a few wine glasses please"

Other 'AW' Books

WINEMAKING

Amateur Winemaker Recipes	£2.50
Commonsense Winemaking	£2.00
Diabetic Winemaking and Brewing	£2.00
First Steps in Winemaking	£2.50
Great Fermentations	£2.50
Making Mead	£1.80
Making Wines Like Those You Buy	£2.50
Modern Winemaking Techniques	£2.50
Progressive Winemaking	£5.95
Quickie Table Wines	£1.00
Recipes for Prizewinning Wines	£2.00
Scientific Winemaking – Made Easy	£2.95
Whys and Wherefores of Winemaking	£2.00
Winemakers Dictionary	£2.95
Winemaking and Brewing	£2.00
Winemaking Simplified	£2.00
Winemaking with Canned and Dried Fruits	£2.00
Winemaking with Concentrates	£2.00
Winemaking with Elderberries	£2.00
Winemaking from your Vines	£2.50
Wines with a Sparkle	£2.50

Worldwide Wine Recipes	£2.00
100 Winemaking Problems Answered	£2.00
130 New Winemaking Recipes	£2.50

BREWING

All About Beer	£2.50
Beer Kits and Brewing	£2.50
The Big Book of Brewing	£3.50
Brewing Beers Like Those You Buy	£2.50
Brewing Better Beers	£2.00
The Happy Brewer	£2.00
Hints on Home Brewing	£1.00
Home Brewed Beers and Stouts	£2.50
Home Brewing for Americans	£2.00

MISCELLANEOUS

Be a Wine and Beer Judge	£1.50
Growing Vines	£2.50
Making Cider	£2.00
Making Inexpensive Liqueurs	£2.50
Think Guitar	£2.50
Vines in your Garden	£1.00
Woodwork for Winemakers	£2.50

Send your orders to: Argus Books Ltd., Wolsey House, Wolsey Road
Hemel Hempstead, Herts., HP2 4SS Telephone: (0442) 41221

INDEX

NOTES

NOTES

NOTES

NOTES

NOTES